Crimson Cross

Uncovering the Mysteries
of the Chinese House Church

by Eugene Bach & Brother Zhu

edited by Minna

CRIMSON CROSS

Uncovering the Mysteries of the Chinese House Church

Fifth Estate, Post Office Box 116,
Blountsville, AL 35031

FIRST EDITION

Cover Design & Layout by Christian

Printed on acid-free paper

Library of Congress Control No: 2012935417

ISBN: 978-1-936533-23-7

Fifth Estate, 2012

For all those who will join God
in what He is doing through
the Chinese House Church

CONTENTS

PREFACE

God wants to take you on a path that you could never think of!

Greetings from the "Heavenly Man." As a follower of Jesus, I am your partner in patiently enduring the suffering that comes to those who belong to His Kingdom. The Bible tells us, "Jesus Christ is the same yesterday and today and forever" (Hebrews 13:8). And Jesus Himself tells the truth: "I am the way, and the truth, and the life. No one comes to the Father except through me" (John 14:6).

Before the God who loves us, I'm sincerely recommending this great book, *Crimson Cross*, to you. I can assure you that if you truly surrender yourself to God's purposes, this book will not only convert your old, wrong concept about being a missionary, but also guide you onto a radical mission path. Thanks be to God!

As you read it, you will be amazed at so many wonderful acts that God is doing in the Chinese church today. The Back to Jerusalem vision is not merely a call to the Chinese church; western believers of this age should also share a part in it. Perhaps your specific plan or commitment differs from mine, but remember, Jesus' Great Commission is for everyone who follows Him: preach this Good News about the Kingdom through the world for a witness to all nations.

O Lord! May your kingdom come down upon China, the Middle East, and Jerusalem! Surely, the time of God to move has come near! Through our Lord Jesus' death on the cross and the power that raised him from the dead, the Holy Spirit will take us step by step into the very destiny to which God has called us in the last days: go and spread Jesus' great love among the nations full of Atheism, Buddhism, and Hinduism and in the Middle East.

With God's truthful words, we can say with full conviction that the Good News about Jesus Christ is going to save all who believe. Both descendants of Ishmael and Isaac can be saved by believing in Jesus' name! Would you accept and respond to God's call for your life, then start to work together with Him?

Brother Yun
February 22, 2012

INTRODUCTION

I was finally able to sit down with the mysterious Brother Ren. He was sitting across from me at a small wooden table and seemed to be in deep thought when he began to tell me about the things that he has seen in China over the past thirty years.

It is not easy to arrange a meeting with Brother Ren. Some would say that it is next to impossible. Brother Ren, also known as the "Flying Finn," can meet with you for dinner one evening, preach a message on the opposite side of the globe before you even wake up the following morning, and be back in time to greet you for lunch. It had taken a lot of planning and nothing short of an act of God to trap him long enough to talk to him about his vast experiences with the underground House Church in China.

Like most people, you've probably never heard of Brother Ren. Keep in mind that in secretive organizations like the CIA, KGB, or PSB, fame and recognition are synonymous with failure. This is also true for Brother Ren. Any fame or advertisement of his achievements would be a major failure, as they would most likely lead to the shutting down of projects and missionary work in many closed countries around the world.

Brother Ren has been the pastor of Brother Yun, more widely known as the Heavenly Man, for many years. He is also the official translator for Brother Yun because he is one of the few Mandarin speakers in the West who can understand Yun's strong rural dialect.

We were sitting on a remote island in Northern Europe. The island, only about one kilometer across with no signs of human life, had no running water or electricity. It was a truly remarkable place, the complete opposite of the crowded and dusty streets of rural China that Brother Ren has called home for over thirty years.

Brother Ren has been responsible for printing and

delivering more than eleven million Bibles in China, organizing the training of more than two hundred thousand Chinese Sunday School teachers, arranging the training of thousands of pastors, evangelists, and missionaries, funneling tens of millions of dollars directly to the mission field, and participating in what may quite possibly be the largest mission movement in the history of mankind.

I started off the interview with, "I know that you have been one of the few people able to print and distribute the Bible in China. How did that happen? How did that start?" He leaned back in his chair and paused for a moment to think, then sat up and excitedly moved to the edge of his seat as he began to tell the story in vivid detail.

What you are about to read is a true story as told by Brother Ren. The facts have been cross-checked and confirmed with other participants in the events mentioned. Never before has this true tale of Christian boldness been written down or told in any formal manner.

> BROTHER REN: It was not easy to get Bibles into China after Deng Xiaoping opened up the nation for international trade in the 1980's. The Bibles were trickling in one by one and it was considered a huge success if one believer in a thousand could get their hands on a Bible. This carried on even in the 1990's. One of the growing trends at the time was bringing Bibles into China in suitcases. Many missionaries and students from around the world began to travel to Hong Kong and cross the border with China to carry in Bibles and drop them off at pre-designated collection points. In those days most Bibles came into Hong Kong from Japan because Japan was one of the few places in Asia where the high-quality paper needed for Bible printing could be purchased.
>
> During the 1980s I was living in Taiwan and preaching the gospel there. The Lord had placed a heavy burden on my heart for China and in the 1990's my family and I moved to Hong Kong. I had taken tour groups from the West into China and was familiar with Hong Kong and southern China. The needs of the church in those days were even greater than today because in many ways it was still in the beginning stages. With so many needs it was hard to

decide where to begin, but the need for Bibles throughout China was so huge that I decided to start there. I became a donkey for Jesus and began to carry Bibles into China. I often took the Bibles into the southern area and dropped them off in places like Guilin.

After carrying Bibles into China for several months, I began to feel challenged by the expense involved. Being a donkey for Jesus was not cheap. I sat down and figured out the actual cost of taking Bibles into China. If you calculated in the cost of printing the Bibles in Japan, shipping them to Hong Kong, paying travel expenses for the courier (such as airfare, food, and lodging), and losing some Bibles to confiscation, it was a very expensive operation. I figured it out to be more than US$50 per Bible—and that was in the 1990s.

God gave me the idea of printing Bibles inside China, but I was a courier, not a printer. Who was I to begin a printing operation? I went to people whom I knew had a history of doing these kinds of projects, such as people from East Gate Mission, Revival Christian Center, and other groups associated with helping Chinese get Bibles. I asked them what they thought about the idea of partnering with me to print Bibles in China. Every time I mentioned the idea I got one of two responses. They either said that they had tried before and it didn't work or they hadn't tried before and didn't want to. The Bible League said that they had just made a large financial investment in an expensive printing press in Japan so printing in China would make that investment obsolete. Many organizations had burned their hands in China and didn't want to try again.

I was disappointed at the results of trying to find a partner who knew what they were doing. I had no clue what to do next, but the Lord would not take the burden from my mind. On one occasion in 1994 I was able to have a meeting with a well-known business owner from Taiwan who owned one of the major skyscrapers in prestigious Causeway Bay, Hong Kong. We met and discussed the idea of printing inside China. The business owner was a Christian and wanted to use his resources to help the church in China. He would later be one of the people who helped get Brother Yun out of China.

The Taiwanese Christian businessman liked the idea of printing Bibles in China and agreed with me that there must be a better way than carrying the Bibles across the border in suitcases. He arranged for his secretary to meet me at the Hong Kong airport, and she gave me the money to begin the process of searching for a way to print Bibles inside China.

From Hong Kong I traveled to Guilin and contacted a professor at one of the local universities who was a good friend of Brother Yun. This is the same professor who spent time living with Brother Yun and painstakingly handwrote Yun's entire testimony on a pad of paper. That pad of paper eventually led to a book known around the world today as *The Heavenly Man*.

"I have someone I would like you to meet," the professor said to me when I saw him in Guilin. In China you don't just look up potential partners in the yellow pages; you are either introduced to them or you don't get any partners at all. With most things in China, it is not about what you know but *who* you know.

The professor thought that it would be beneficial for me to meet his friend. He knew what I was up to and knew the risks involved with printing Bibles in China, so he connected me with someone who he thought would be experienced enough to help me tackle the dangerous task. I needed someone who could help me navigate the underground world of illegal activity in China.

When I met with the professor's friend for the first time he looked like he was straight out of a movie. The man looked like a CIA agent. Just by looking at him you could tell that he was used to living on the other side of authority. There was something that was very shady about him. He was wearing a hunting vest, his hair was pulled back into a thick black pony tail, and he just looked like someone who seemed to be fully aware of everything going on around him. When he walked into the room I thought that I had been compromised. I thought that the professor had told the wrong person and now China's Public Security Bureau had assigned this man to take me down.

"This is my friend Simon [not his real name]," the professor said as I reached out to shake his hand. Even though I had my suspicions, I quickly found myself falling victim to Simon's quick wit and charm. However, I remained very cautious the first time that I met him and chose not to share with him the idea for printing Bibles.

I soon went back to Hong Kong, but often traveled to Guilin. Many foreigners liked to take Bibles to Guangzhou and their favorite place to stay was The Garden Hotel. Because of this, it was heavily watched and most of the rooms were wired. The hotel was a gold mine for the Chinese authorities because many foreign guests would talk about their ideas and projects, carelessly mentioning names of coworkers. All of this information was thus made available for the Chinese authorities to collect and exploit. This was one of the reasons I chose Guilin for my meetings instead of more traditional places like Guangzhou or Shenzhen. Guilin was frequented by tourists and government officials, rather than conspicuous missionaries.

On one of my trips to Guilin the phone in my hotel room rang soon after I had arrived. I answered the phone and it was Simon. I wondered how he knew I was in town because I hadn't told anyone that I was going to Guilin. No one should have known which hotel I was staying at, let alone the very room I was in! Immediately I was suspicious.

"Ni hao," I said as a general greeting. Simon invited me to come to his home for dinner, a huge honor in China. I was still suspicious. He seemed to know too much. I thought that dinner might just be a ruse to trap me, but there was another part of me that said to trust him. My policy was to follow the old Ronald Reagan strategy of "trust, but verify." I accepted the invitation.

I took a taxi to the location he had told me to go to, but I didn't go directly to the address. Instead I asked the driver to keep driving. We drove a few blocks down the road and then I walked around the area, looking for anything suspicious and for possible escape routes if I needed to leave in a hurry.

Simon would later tell me that he had contacts in

the hotel I was staying in who had been instructed to look out for me and alert him if they saw me. I didn't know it then, but Simon would soon play a huge part in my life and we would grow to be very close friends.

When I went into the home, the house was filled with some of the most amazing smells I have ever smelled in my life. Simon was an amazing world class chef! He warmly welcomed me into his home and showed me around. It is not easy to explain, but we had an immediate connection. Simon was a new friend, but it felt that I had known him for years.

I had never eaten such good food in all my life! Simon was able to work magic with food and put together flavors that danced across your tongue. After dinner, Simon showed me his photography awards and shared stories with me about his family's grand and royal history. As the evening came to a close, Simon invited me to return and spend time with his family.

I later went and spent time with his parents and grandparents. I am usually very secretive about my vision and projects for China, but with Simon's family I shared exactly what God had called me to do. I shared with them about my ideas regarding the movement of God in the world and what I felt God had told me regarding the future of China and the Chinese underground House Church. Upon hearing my story, Simon's grandmother took me by the hand, looked intensely in my eyes, and asked me one of the strangest questions I had ever been asked: "Would you like to be adopted by our family?"

I heard the words that she said, but immediately thought that I must not be able to understand her Chinese. She asked again, "Would you like to be adopted by our family?" As she said it again, I realized that I did in fact understand the words coming out of her mouth, they just didn't make sense to me. Why would I want to be adopted? I was more than forty years old. The time to adopt me was over. Besides, I had my own mother, father, and grandparents.

I began to tell myself that maybe the family needed money or some "golden goose" to help their family with financial problems and saw that this foreigner might provide them with a way out of poverty. I took that opportunity to reiterate that I was only a missionary who was financially poor and had nothing to offer. The grandmother looked at me. You could tell from the expression on her face that my financial status had never even crossed her mind.

The grandmother was persistent. She felt that God was telling her to bring me into her family. I also felt the presence of the Lord and humbly accepted their great honor. Together we went through the entire official process. I filled out all of the paper work and upon completion we had an official ceremony marking the time when I became an adopted member of Simon's family.

From that day on, Simon and I became inseparable ministry partners. Whenever people saw us and asked who we were, I jokingly replied that we were brothers. This was funny to everyone who witnessed it, because it was obvious that this Chinese man and a Western European were not brothers. We would always tell people that we had different mothers, but the same Father.

Simon became my partner in crime to print the Bible in China. He turned out to be an amazingly resourceful man.

Once we decided to print the Bible in China we quickly arrived at the same conclusion: it couldn't be done. But we just continued to believe in God. I began to bring the Chinese Bible to Simon in pieces. Simon had been a photography instructor and had many students who had graduated and started their own businesses. Many of those businesses were major photo shops. Piece by piece we desired to build an archive of photographic negatives of the Bible for printers.

Simon's former students were everywhere and they all welcomed us with warm and open arms. Everywhere we went Simon would joke with them as he introduced me as his brother. After the formalities of meeting with the photography shop owners, we began to talk about our objectives. Eventually we were able to find a place to make the film for the Bible printing. After some time, I received a phone call letting me know that the film was complete. The film was rolled up in newspaper when I picked it up.

Once we had the film in our hands, we began to meet with each of the students again to see if we could get the Bible printed. When the students saw us coming they were excited, I think for two reasons. One, they loved Simon. He really knew how to make a grand entrance and make his presence known. He didn't have much money, but no one knew that. Simon was able to present himself in a way that impressed people and made them think that he had a lot of money. He only knew two English words and he used them all the time, which made a big impression on the rural Chinese who thought Simon must have been really cultured to be able to speak English. Little did they know that the only two phrases Simon knew were "no problem," and "sit down please." He used those two phrases all the time and was really good at pronouncing them well. The other reason I think they were excited to see us is that they saw a foreigner, i.e. an opportunity to make money. One by one, we shared with them our desire to print the Bible. Each time we told one of them, their heart would sink and they would hang their head in disappointment. "Dear honorable teacher, you are always welcome in our place. We would do anything to please you and assist you, but we are unable to help you on this project," they would often say in reply.

I understood their challenge. If they agreed to help us, their livelihood would be in danger. At that time a law had just come out that said that anyone caught printing a Bible would be arrested, their business confiscated, and they would be given a minimum of seven years in prison. We visited twelve to fifteen different photography shops, all of which were owned by Simon's former students, but every one of them was reluctant to help us. Even though I understood, I still found the fact that they wouldn't print the Bible a bit perplexing. I mean, we were traveling in the kinds of places that I had never been to before in the interior of China. These printers said they were not able to print Bibles illegally because the risk was too high, but most of them printed many illegal things that I considered to be much more dangerous than printing the Bible. They were printing pornography, anti-government and anti-Communist materials. Personally, I thought that those materials were more damning for the government than a mere religious book.

More time passed and we visited all potential printing places Simon could think of. We traveled to places far from the city center and met with people who really knew the underground printing world well. We had searched high and low and came up empty handed. We felt that this vision was directly from the Lord and were really confused. If God wanted us to do this, then why were all of the doors closing on us? If God truly gave us the vision to print these Bibles in China, then why did every road lead to a dead end?

Simon had returned to the city. We were standing in the town square and a sense of depression descended upon me. I looked at Simon and said, "Simon, we have done all that we can do. There is nothing more than can be done."

"We haven't done *all* that we can do," he replied.

"Of course we have. Is there a place that we have not tried? Do you know someone else that we haven't talked to yet? It seems that everyone has turned us away because it is just too dangerous to print Bibles in China."

"No. We have not tried *that* place."

I turned to look at the place he was pointing to. I saw a massive building within walking distance with a big red banner draped across the front. As I began to make sense of the bold Chinese characters on the banner, I realized what Simon was proposing was suicide!

"We can't go there!" I said quickly, "No way!"

"Why not?" He replied.

I looked at his face expecting there to be a smirk or laugh. Maybe he was trying to lighten the mood from all of our disappointments, but as I looked at him I realized that he had a look of seriousness in his eyes. He wasn't joking.

I looked back up at the banner. The sign indicated that the building in front of us was the official printing headquarters for the Chinese government.

"How can we honestly tell the Lord that we have done all that we could if we have not?" he said indignantly. "I cannot go to the Lord and tell him in good conscience that I have done everything in my power to do what I believe He has called us to do. There is a printing press right there in front of us, all we have to do is try."

He was serious and had to be stopped. "Simon! Look at that building. It is the official printing press. Take a good long look at those guards. If we go over there with our request, it is possible they will shoot us. This is not funny. We are talking about a serious situation here."

Simon had made up his mind. He believed strongly that a believer who has been given a task from the Lord such as this one must put all of his or her trust in the Lord. Only walking by faith will allow us to see the glory of the Lord.

I tried to reason with Simon, but he compelled me to trust in the Lord. I was encouraged by his faith, but grounded with reason. As I looked at Simon, I knew that this was something that he felt strongly about and he would go into that building with or without me. On the other hand, I felt that it was not only hopeless to try, but we were needlessly endangering our lives and work.

It was at that moment that I wondered what kind of family I had been adopted into. I was reluctant to go, but as I looked back at Simon he looked at me with a smirk on his face, patted me on the back, and said his famous phrase, "no problem."

Together we walked to the main gate. We didn't have an appointment with anyone (you don't just walk up to one of these places unannounced). Simon boldly approached one of the guards—acting as if he had every right to walk into any top-security area in China—and said, "Hello, I need to speak with the director. Can you please let him know that I am here?"

The guards did exactly as they were told without missing a beat. They called the director on his direct line. "Sir, there are two gentlemen here who have arrived without an appointment and would like to see you," the guard said. I could hear the voice on the other end of the phone reply, "Send them up to the fourth floor, I am waiting for them." I stood still. The guard motioned for us to go on up. I looked over at Simon in disbelief, but he didn't look back. He was acting like things were going along just as he had envisioned.

We arrived on the fourth floor and walked into the director's office. The office looked as large as a full-size basketball court. It was decorated in hand-carved rosewood and made a very imposing impression on everyone who entered that office door. I could tell right away that this was a guy with enough power to have us arrested on the spot. I didn't know exactly how to start the conversation. I mean, how do you begin? "Hello sir, I know that you are employed by the government to print its most important propaganda in this country of more than one-billion people, but would it also be possible for you to print this here Bible that has been outlawed?" What we were doing was absurd in every way.

"Hello, hello," he said warmly. "Please come in and sit. How may I help you?"

"We have come to see about having this book printed," Simon explained to him. Coming from behind I slowly unwrapped the Bible that I had been carefully concealing. This was the point of no return. Once I handed him the Bible and he saw what we were doing, there would be no explaining our way out of this.

I slowly reached across to give him the Bible. He took it, looked at the cover, and ran his hands over the surface. He opened the Bible and flipped through the pages quickly, as if to examine the quality of the binding and to gauge the paper thickness. He then turned to a certain passage in Genesis. He flipped through the chapters in Genesis deliberately as if he knew exactly what he was looking for. I stood there in shock as he began to read a story from the book of Genesis! He read aloud the story of Ishmael. After he read the passage he asked us, "are you Christians?"

The room was silent. His question echoed in the room as well as in our minds. It only took a few seconds to answer, but the silence seemed to linger for an eternity.

"Yes," we said, refusing to deny the name of Christ, but still confused as to what would happen next.

"Well then, doesn't that make you sons of Abraham?" he asked as a matter of fact. We nodded our heads in agreement. "So am I. I too am a son of Abraham," he said as he handed back the Bible, indicating that he was actually a Muslim. Immediately he asked, "How many books do you want me to print?" I was not able to answer. I was in a state of shock. "No matter, I will call you when I have the sample ready." We shook hands, turned, and walked out the door—just like that!

God is amazing, but the miracles were not done yet. Two weeks later I received a call telling me that my package was finished. I met Simon and we traveled there together. I arranged to get a small fold up bag to carry the book or books in and also had stuffed my pockets with the needed cash because I had made it clear that we were not paying for the samples until the product was complete. I didn't want a situation where I paid for a project that was later reported to the authorities so the printer could take my money while I was detained by the police.

When we arrived at the printing headquarters we met with the Muslim fellow and he led us down to a storage area. He walked up to these two massive doors and opened them. I almost fell over—the room was filled with Bibles! The stacks were higher than I have ever seen in my entire life. There were thousands of them.

I dropped the small bag that I brought to carry them in, it was useless now. I couldn't fit twenty thousand Bibles in my pitiful duffel bag. We now had a huge load of Bibles in China sitting in the warehouse of the Communist printing headquarters! There was no way on earth we could get these Bibles out of the building undetected. I looked over at Simon and asked, "Great! What in the world are we going to do now?" Simon just smiled and replied, "No problem."

Simon had a friend during elementary school who had sat next to him in class. As I said earlier, in China it's not about what you know, but *who* you know; referred to in Chinese as *guanxi*. Simon pulled out a phone and called his old classmate. I didn't know it then, but his old school chum was the commanding officer of the entire southern China armed forces. I could hear Simon using very polite language when talking with him over the phone. The commanding officer talked with him and after some time asked Simon, "Simon, what is it I can do for you?"

"Well, we happen to have a very sensitive document of a secure nature here at the Communist printing headquarters and we would like some assistance in getting it to another location."

I could not hear the reply, but they talked for a little longer and then Simon hung up the phone. I asked him what his friend said and Simon smiled at me and said, "He said, 'no problem.'"

Within minutes a huge military truck came barreling our way. There were three men sitting in the truck and two men hanging on both sides. They backed the truck up to the warehouse and began to load all of the "sensitive, top secret" documents. We didn't even lift a finger; the soldiers loaded it all on the truck in no time. Simon told the driver that we needed the "sensitive" materials to be taken to the airport. The distance from the printing headquarters to the airport was thirty to forty miles (38-64km). During that time in China there were many road blocks on the way to the airport to check documentation. Though were several road blocks between us and the airport, we were never stopped once. As we drove up to the checkpoints, the police and soldiers saluted us and allowed us to pass without ever checking the cargo.

When we arrived at the airport we had another problem: there was no way to fly this cargo to Beijing on any of the shipping routes. We had looked into all the different options and nothing was working out at the airport. Simon looked at me when I was at the peak of my frustration and said in perfect English, "No problem."

While he was in school, something I believe God had planned all along, on one side of him sat the future commanding officer of the southern armed forces in China and on the other side sat a boy who would become the director of the China's largest cargo company. Simon called his other friend and told him he had "top secret" military cargo that he needed to be flown to Beijing. His friend said that he would arrange it right away. Within minutes we had the military truck pull onto the tarmac of the heavily-guarded airport.

I was standing below the plane just in awe. I had never seen the nose of a plane open up like that. The truck pulled up to the plane and the soldiers worked together with the crew to load up every single box of Bibles. I was not allowed to fly with the cargo, so I walked inside the airport and got on the next flight to Beijing.

I called Brother Yun and our other friends who still live in China today, to come and help us at the Beijing airport. There were thirteen people in Beijing waiting for the plane to land. I wish I had brought my camera! These Chinese brothers were hiding behind trees and watching the planes intently as they came in, trying to see if the plane with the Bibles was landing. It was late in the evening and Brother Yun and the rest of the team had brought several vehicles to help with transportation. To get into the cargo area, they had to register their names. They all registered with fake names.

Small vehicles came pulling a train of carts loaded with the Bibles. Sitting next to the driver of one small vehicle was Simon. He was just smiling and laughing as if we were all having the best time of our lives. I opened the back door of one of the carts loaded with Bibles. As I opened the door I noticed the big red Chinese Characters for "Bible" had been written on the box. I looked at the other boxes and they too had been written on. All of the boxes had the words *Shengjing* (Bible) written on them in enormous bright red ink. Immediately I thought we had been compromised.

"Simon! Look! Someone has written the word Bible on all of these boxes."

Simon began laughing. This guy was really having the best time of his entire life.

"I did that," Simon said. "As the soldiers were loading and unloading God's Word, I took out a red marker and put the words 'Bible' on every box."

"Why? Why would you do something like that?"

"Because," he explained, "I wanted to see if God was truly with us."

"Please do not ever do that again."

Before morning came, we had loaded all of the Bibles into privately-owned vehicles and were able to ship them out all over China to Christians that were hungry to have the Word of God. Not one Bible was lost from that operation.

The miracles of course did not stop there. They happen every time we do a Bible printing. A few months later after that miraculous airlift, the situation changed when one of the delivery company workers was loading Bibles and a box broke open, revealing the illegal contents. Once again, Simon called his friend and asked for a temporary shelter for our "sensitive items." The army trucks came and picked up all of the cargo and took it to an ammunition depot guarded by around fifteen thousand troops. I have often wondered if the government will ever know what critical role they play in the domestic Bible printing we continue to do to this day.

1

THE MIDDLE KINGDOM MODERNIZES

As Brother Yun and others representing the Chinese House Church and the Back to Jerusalem vision travel the globe to introduce people to what God is doing in China, many questions arise, such as, "What is the 'House Church'? What is its origin? Where is it going? What is it like?"

At the same time, there is a great deal of misinformation going around causing confusion abroad. Some of it is spread maliciously for personal gain, but most is spread ignorantly by unwitting foreigners or overseas Chinese who have had the wool pulled over their eyes by the Chinese government. Some would even have us believe that there is no House Church in China! Others that they are just a ragtag group of unorganized country bumpkins making bumbling and misguided attempts at preaching the gospel (these stories tend to come from groups who value how many advanced theological degrees a pastor has over his calling from God). Still others will go as far as to say that the House Church is an outdated nuisance to Christianity in mainland China and is irrelevant because there is now complete freedom of religion in the country (which is the official party line fed to many unsuspecting foreigners).A main purpose for this book is to dispel such rumors hopefully once and for all.

China is a place of mystery and fascinating discoveries. In the minds of people the world over, the very name of this country invokes images of dragon dances, clanging gongs, the Forbidden City, and rich culture. The Chinese are a proud people with a long history that has left fingerprints all over the development of humankind.

Not only is the history of the Chinese people rich and vibrant, but the future of the Chinese people has never looked better. Today China is considered to be the rising red star in the

East that is beginning to challenge the world's largest superpower. Children across the world from India to the US are starting learn Mandarin Chinese as their second language and previously scoffed-at Chinese traditional medicine is being embraced worldwide.

China's rapid growth can be seen everywhere. It is a major issue in both the news and political debates around the world. Those who travel to China end up finding cities that are growing faster than travel guidebooks can keep up with.

However, behind China's rapid economic growth is a movement that cannot be seen on a guided tour of Beijing's ancient streets and monuments. You will not learn about it while studying Chinese at the Beijing Language and Cultural University, nor will it be addressed in western political debates, but the movement is one of the largest in the world and is shaping every facet of China today.

The underground house churches of China (collectively referred to as the Chinese House Church) are exploding at a phenomenal rate. The Chinese church is one of the greatest miracles in modern history. Never before have so many people in such a short time left one belief system for another without a hostile takeover. Lives are being completely transformed every day in China by nothing more than the gospel of Jesus Christ and the display of His miraculous power. Many experts claim that there are about thirty thousand people coming to Christ in China every day. That is a shockingly large number of people, coming from every age group, ethnic group, demographic, and income level.

As China rises in global economic prowess, the Chinese are making increasingly more money and enjoying more freedoms than ever before, but true happiness and fulfillment are managing to evade them. The expectation of finding happiness in riches mixed with atheistic materialism are leaving many people feeling empty and without purpose. China has indeed become a world superpower, but her fast-paced economic development has left many people searching for a joy and purpose that cannot be purchased in the local market nor copied and sold beside Rolex knockoffs in the back streets of Shenzhen.

Chinese parents are scraping money together to put their children through the very best schools in China or abroad so that they will have a chance at grabbing some of the new money in China's burgeoning business world. The better schools allow children to have special opportunities not available by any other means in China, so doting parents are more than willing to do anything to get them into those schools. They often go into debt, work twelve-hour days every day of the week, and pour all that they have into their one child so he or she may take advantage of every opportunity for career advancement. It is thus a serious blow to the entire family when their little emperor or empress becomes a Christian, leaves the competitive rat race, and forsakes all to serve Jesus Christ as their Lord and Savior.

Amy (not her real name) is a prime example. She was an only child and the first in her family to attend a university. Both of her parents worked for the Communist government. Her mother was an auditor and her father a family planning official who enforced China's infamous one-child policy. They used all of their resources together to put their daughter through one of the best schools in Jiangxi Province and Amy eventually received a degree in international business. However, during her time in university she was introduced to Jesus Christ and eventually became a Christian, and a radical one at that.

Amy left the big cities—ripe with opportunities for a girl with her prestigious background—and went to work for a small hotel in the rural area of Guangxi Province instead. She did so in order to preach the gospel to the ethnic minorities living in that area. Her reputation began to grow as she preached the gospel to everyone she came in contact with. Soon her passion for the gospel grabbed the attention of some underground House Church leaders who wanted to meet with her. Two representatives visited her at the rural hotel she was working at and heard about her vision to preach the gospel. They were surprised to find that Amy did not even know it was illegal to preach Christ in China. Even as a Chinese, she had never heard of the underground house churches. Amy quit working at the hotel that very day and dedicated her life to serving beside underground Chinese Christians. In only a couple of days she found herself in Sichuan Province helping the earthquake victims through the efforts of the underground House Church networks.

Amy later traveled to another city to help the underground House Church and moved in with a foreign missionary family. In love with Jesus but completely unaware of what was or was not illegal in her own country, she began to go out in the streets and proclaim the message of salvation soon after her arrival. She then made evangelistic tracts and handed them out throughout the city.

Thinking it would be helpful for people who got saved through the tracts and needed more information, she wrote the exact contact information of the western missionary family on the back of every tract. Needless to say, the western missionary was alarmed and told Amy to act wisely in a country where it is illegal to proselytize.

The underground House Church movement is not only mysterious to people outside of China, but even to those like Amy who live there. A singer very well-known inside China named Zhao Ming became famous when he and his family won the Chinese version of "American Idol" by singing a Christian song about loving one's family. He went on tour in Finland with Brother Yun, a well-known Chinese evangelist whose life has been documented in the popular book *The Heavenly Man*. During that time Zhao Ming read Yun's book and was blown away by the torture and sacrifice that Brother Yun had endured in China for being a follower of Christ. "I have never heard before of those things happening to Christian believers in China," Zhao Ming replied.

The fact is, every single day thousands of people are coming to Christ in China and the vast majority are doing it illegally. There are an estimated 130 to 150 million believers in China at the time of writing and the majority of them belong to the illegal underground churches.

People all over the world are asking questions like: What is the Chinese House Church? Why is that term even used? How can you prove it even exists? Who does it consist of? Where is it? How did it start? How does it continue to grow at such an astronomical rate? Why are the Chinese experiencing a revival when other countries on their borders are not?

This book will attempt to answer each of these questions and demystify the Chinese House Church. The authors hope that anyone who reads this book will be able to gain a basic understanding of what exactly the underground House Church of China is.

As the story unfolds, examples and personal testimonies from underground Chinese Christians will be included whenever possible to help better explain certain ideas and concepts. It is important that the Chinese themselves be able to explain what they have witnessed in their nation in their own words. None of these stories have been shared in a book before and many of them have never left the borders of China. Although these stories are factual, the names of people and places have often been changed to protect the safety of individuals who are still living or serving in China.

Many of the laws and restrictions on Christians in China are not easy to explain and can cause controversy. There are not many official laws restricting Christians that are specifically spelled out the same way they are enforced. The reader must also keep in mind that China is a huge country where certain laws are enforced in differing degrees from Province to Province and even city to city. A believer living in Beijing may tell you that the laws are such and such, but a believer living in Chengdu may argue that the laws are different, and yet still a Christian in Lhasa, Tibet will say something entirely different about Chinese law from the other two.

Chinese politics are simply not easily understood by outsiders. The average tourist quickly discovers this when they try to go between Hong Kong and the mainland. What country is Hong Kong a part of? China? Then why can an American or European go there for three months without a visa but needs to pay an exorbitant price for a mere thirty-day visa to cross the border into China proper? What kind of unified country has customs and immigration offices between two of its own regions? Another example is the issue of international drivers. It is no problem for most foreigners to drive in Hong Kong; they just need to use their foreign driver's license. However, just across the border in Shenzhen foreigners are not allowed to drive until they go through the complicated and expensive process to get a Chinese driver's license. On paper Hong Kong is indeed a part of China, yet the laws, banking system, currencies, and to a large degree the government systems are all completely different. It is officially referred to as one country with two systems, but the difference on both sides of the border is quite remarkable. Macau is also a part of China that has completely different laws and policies than that of China or Hong Kong.

Even more baffling is China's relationship with Taiwan. China says that Taiwan belongs to China and the UN also takes this stance. In fact, the vast majority of the world—the United States included—makes this same claim, yet Chinese officials cannot set foot on Taiwan's soil without permission from the independent democratic Taiwanese government.

Taiwan also has its own government, laws, banks, and currency. It even has its own military that is primarily set up to defend itself against the very country that claims to own it. Much to China's outrage, America even provides Taiwan with highly secretive military equipment and training, also frequently carrying out join military exercises.

If all those issues seem complicated and confusing, so too is the situation of Christians in mainland China. The laws, practices, and degrees of enforcement are different from province to province and also change from year to year. There will be people familiar with China who will undoubtedly try to challenge the authenticity of some of this book's content, even citing their own experiences for validation, but let the reader beware of anyone who is considered to be a "China expert." The term itself is an oxymoron.

What China's underground house churches are experiencing today is a combination of many different factors. One significant factor is that today's Chinese Christians are standing on the shoulders of those who sacrificed their lives in China many years ago. Today's spiritual explosion is the fruit of a seed that sat underground unseen by the outside world for many years. This seed fought to survive through the cold harsh winter, was watered by the blood of a myriad of martyrs, and has today grown into a mighty tree bearing so much fruit that the branches are bent and almost breaking under the weight.

At the same time it is interesting to note that the very people who brought the gospel to China and sacrificed so much were the very people that needed to leave before the seed would fully sprout. Foreign missionaries provided much of the support and strength for the Chinese believers in the early days. The same strength and faith that contributed to the revivals of today was also a hindrance to the spiritual growth of the Chinese church in that time.

Missionaries brought with them doctrinal and cultural systems that crippled the growth of the indigenous Chinese church. Control of the church through monetary means is rarely talked about in the Bible, but because of flawed human nature, even the most saintly missionaries often wielded the power of money over the power of the Holy Spirit.

The early church in China was fascinated by the ingenuity, education, and wealth of the foreign missionaries. Since the majority of the missionaries were highly skilled in trades like medicine, they were considered by many to be superior. Even some missionaries considered themselves superior to the poor heathens they came to proselytize. However, the Chinese Christians didn't realize that these seemingly superior qualities like knowledge and wealth were not due to nationality or ethnicity, rather they were the byproducts of cultures massively influenced by the gospel and teachings of Jesus Christ. There were no differences between the missionaries and the Chinese in the human sense. The missionaries were just as vulnerable to disease, needed daily nourishment, and were subject to the same temptations of any human being. The missionaries and Chinese were both initially lost sinners in need of a Savior. The difference was in their cultural backgrounds. The western missionary by and large had been raised in a society formed by biblical ethics and morality. The Judeo-Christian understanding of the fear of the Lord being the beginning of wisdom had helped to create a society that greatly benefited all its members. On the other hand, Chinese culture had been covered in darkness for generations under the influence of Buddhism, Taoism, and Animism. This antithesis of light and biblical truth made a dog-eat-dog society of degradation and brokenness where people were constantly oppressed.

Today institutions of higher learning around the world often propound these ignorant and godless teachings under the auspicious title "wisdom of the East," attempting to mask their religious nature as mere ancient wisdom. Far from it, the religions of the East are responsible for a great deal of the suffering that continues not only in China, but throughout Asia to this day. As international test scores in recent years have proved, the Chinese are in no way intellectually inferior to their western counterparts. Rather it is the errors of these dark religions that have counteracted their extremely resourceful and productive natures. It was the Light of the World that the Chinese saw in the missionaries of yesterday and that same Light is now piercing through the darkness of China today.

China's Christian population is currently growing along with their economic influence, medical capabilities, educational development, technological breakthroughs, and even refinement of their leisure activities. And along with the growth of everything else in the country, China is becoming increasingly engaged in world missions. The Chinese church is beginning to send out missionary teams to the most dangerous regions of Southeast and Central Asia, the Middle East, and Africa. They feel called to carry out the Great Commission in areas that the western world has largely neglected

31

or cannot even go to if they wanted to. Chinese Christians are specifically targeting the 10/40 Window, which refers to that part of the eastern hemisphere north of the equator between the ten and forty degree latitudes.

This vision is not unique to the Chinese, but stems from the Great Commission as given to the first century church. What makes this vision sound so novel today is that many churches in the West have lost it. In many ways the current western missionary effort is feeding on itself, with many mission organizations becoming massive self-feeding mechanisms constantly trying to create a new fad movement. Like much of the western church itself, missions has become a big industry stuck doing the same things over and over again, but marketing them differently each time. The hottest new mission strategy becomes obsolete soon after it makes it on a Power Point presentation, but is then just chopped up are reworked into something that sounds more fresh for the next mission conference.

Once a big name walks out on stage with a new idea, catchy slogan, or clever missions idiom, we all want to buy the book and organizations the world over basically copy and repackage it with their own logo prominently displayed. This may raise some financial support, but often does very little to actually make an impact for the advancement of the Kingdom. Missions seminars quickly turn into something akin to a high school pep rally and money raised on "Missions Sunday" ends up going more to the domestic side of comfort enhancement than for true international outreach to the lost.

This harsh evaluation of the common current procedure among Western missionary efforts may seem sacrilegious, but after one has read a plethora of new books, attended numerous meetings, and read years of emails, it becomes apparent that most westerners are focused on the *thought* of doing something good rather than actually doing it. The sad truth is, the only thing tangible about many of the western missions organizations today is the money that they raise and the shiny new offices they spend it on.

That all being said, China still has many things to learn from western missionaries. For generations, the West has been sending its young men and women to live, serve, and die in the most unforgiving foreign lands imaginable. The western church has done and is still doing many wonderful things for missions that shouldn't be drowned out by the circus of strategists trying to market the newest missions trend. The Chinese need all the tools westerners can give them in order to tackle the daunting task God has placed before them.

A Christian missions strategist now living in Dallas, Texas who is helping with placement of Chinese missionaries sat in a restaurant one evening in 2011 and reflected on his own missionary experience, "I remember going to a missions conference where a famous missionary had come to recruit missionaries in the 1980s. The missionary stood up and began to talk about being seriously alarmed about the church in the West and the growing lack of interest for missionary work. He implored us to pray for the church in the West because there was a growing trend of young people rejecting a life of missions and, in his mind, if the West did not send the missionaries the world would be lost."

He paused as he remembered the anxiety of that time and how ignorant people were of the sovereign God. "Little did that missionary know," he continued, "that God was rising up a church in a country that the rest of the world had written off as a completely lost mission field, thinking it would have to be restarted in the future when it country re-opened. Little did he know that God had plans to raise up a church in China and send more missionaries to the Middle East, Southeast and Central Asia, and Africa than had ever been sent in the history of mankind."

China's budding missionary movement was born out of a church that is largely unknown to people around the world. There is still great confusion about what God is doing behind the "bamboo curtain," but it isn't drastically different than other movements of God in history. Not unlike the past missionary movements of the West, China's surge of missionary activity has been born out of revival fires. There are many similarities between the revivals in China and those that have taken place around the world in recent history, one of them being an intense passion for global evangelism that has sparked multiple missionary endeavors.

There are also many characteristics that are unique to the Chinese church. As will be seen, there are many pearls unique to the Chinese House Church that were formed under intense pressure from conflict, suffering, and persecution. Chinese Christians like to say that the history of China runs red, like the crimson blood that was shed on the cross for man's sin. China's cross is crimson, as if stained with the blood of the countless saints who died for her church to rise. This is the story of that rise.

May your faith be challenged and your hearts set aflame for Christ as you read about God's tremendous work in the Chinese House Church.

2

ROOTS OF CHINESE CHRISTIANITY

Our goal is to lift the veil of the underground House Church movement in China so that the world can look inside and see some of the characteristics that are unique to the Chinese church and have contributed to the world's largest revival and mission movement. We want to help readers understand the Chinese House Church and what God is currently doing in the Middle Kingdom. In order to do so, it is important to know the history that shaped the Chinese people and their churches into what they are today. Although it would be impossible to give a comprehensive account of China's long and rich history, the next three chapters will give a brief overview of the development of Christianity in China and provide the historical backdrop for the Chinese House Church movement. The following overview of Christianity in China makes no attempt to be exhaustive, as there are already many great books that go into detail on the subject. Those interested in more thorough accounts of Chinese church history may see the endnotes for further references.

One of Beijing's most popular tourist attractions, the image of which has ironically become a symbol of the Communist nation's capital, is the Temple of Heaven. Foreign Christians who tour the sight are often surprised to learn that the purpose of the temple (*Tiantan*, literally "Altar of Heaven") was to offer sacrificial worship to *Shangdi* (the God of Heaven) in prayer for a good harvest. This temple was completed in A.D. 1420 as part of the Ming Dynasty's attempt to reinstate long-lost *Shangdi* worship practices. Once a year at the winter solstice China's emperor would come to the temple to offer prayers and animal sacrifices to the God of Heaven. After fasting for three days, he would take a tablet with the inscription "Heavenly Sovereign *Shangdi*" on it and place it on a throne in the Hall of Prayer for Good Harvests. While bulls were being sacrificed outside the hall he would intercede on behalf of his nation. This ritual was known as the "Great Sacrifice" and was even referred to by Confucius, who recognized that its true meaning had been lost generations before his time.[1] Although it had turned into nothing more than an empty ritual early on in Chinese history, the practice continued even through China's last imperial dynasty.

This means that the ancient Chinese knew of a merciful God who heard their prayers thousands of years before Confucianism, Taoism, Buddhism, or Communism even existed. Monotheistic faith was not brought to China by western imperialists, as is taught today in China, but had existed in China's ancient past.[2] The wave of Chinese coming to faith in the one True God in our time is really a return to the nation's most ancient spiritual roots.

The oldest existing Chinese records date from the Shang Dynasty (1600-1046 B.C.). These first archeologically verifiable records of Chinese history, known as oracle bones, were written on tortoise shells and cow bones. They mention *Shangdi* as the one Supreme God who ruled over all other spirits and had control over the weather, harvests, and the outcome of battles. The Chinese characters on the oracle bones are interesting in themselves because they contain references to pre-Flood biblical history and theological concepts. One of the clearest examples is the ancient character for "boat," which combines the pictographs for "eight," "mouth" (referring to people), and "ship" or "vessel." There were exactly eight persons on board Noah's Ark. Though the interpretation is debated by some, it seems quite clear that this character makes a reference to Noah's Ark.[3]

This begs the obvious question, "What happened?" When Protestant missionaries first landed on Chinese soil they found a

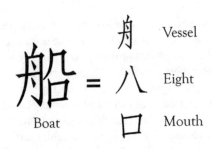

船 = 舟 Vessel
Boat 八 Eight
口 Mouth

people totally lost in darkness, so when had they forgotten about *Shangdi*? At the outset of the Zhou Dynasty (1045-256 B.C.) it was decided that knowledge of *Shangdi* was too high for commoners and anyone other than the emperor was forbidden from worshiping Him. It was from this point onward that sacrifices to *Shangdi* were limited to once a year and could only be carried out by the emperor, who was given the new title "Son of Heaven." Although most likely a political move to solidify allegiance to the new dynasty, the end result was a vast nation looking for something to worship. That void would be filled a few hundred years later by Confucian ancestor worship, Taoism, and an idolatrous form of Buddhism unlike what first came out of India.[1]

Evidence of any belief in God doesn't appear again in Chinese history until the Han Dynasty (206 B.C.-A.D. 226). In recent years stone carvings on Han tombs dating from A.D. 86 were discovered in Xuzhou.[4] These artifacts depict what appear to be stories from both the Old and New Testaments. One carving looks very much like a nativity scene complete with angels flying over the baby in a manger. Although it can't be proven without a doubt, these carvings could very well be evidence that someone from the first generation church made it all the way to China.

Speculation turns to solid fact by the time of the 7th century after Christ. Today in Xian stands the remains of a stele from the Tang Dynasty (A.D. 618-907) that gives an official account of a Christian presence in China. The Nestorian Tablet, inscribed with the date A.D. 781, records the first arrival of the "Religion of Light of the West" as taking place in A.D. 635 via the Silk Road. Alopen, a leader from the Nestorian Church, came from Persia with a syncretistic version of the gospel tailored to please the Taoist Chinese. Nestorianism was a heretical form of Christianity that denied Christ's human and divine nature could coexist in one entity, so the gospel these missionaries presented was questionable. Nevertheless the tablet states their belief in a Creator God, the Fall in Eden, the virgin birth, and the crucifixion of Jesus. In some form at least, the name of Christ was finally proclaimed within China's borders and was even well received by Tang royalty. Perhaps the Nestorians' biggest contribution to the gospel in China was the first Chinese translation of the New Testament, completed in the ninth century. Although there were times when Nestorian converts numbered in the tens of thousands, by and large their growth was severely hampered by their monastic way of life which brooded suspicion among the locals. Their success as a mission ebbed and flowed until the arrival of Roman Catholic missionaries in the thirteenth century.[5]

The Franciscan Friar John of Monte Corvino was the first Catholic missionary to set foot on Chinese soil. During his thirty-year ministry in Beijing he baptized over six thousand converts and translated the New Testament and Psalms into Mongolian, the language of the Mongols ruling China at the time. With the fall of the Mongolian Yuan Dynasty in 1368, Christianity again vanished from the scene.

The founding of the Jesuits—often referred to as Roman Catholic shock troops—brought on a global wave of Catholic evangelism. These men set sail with European explorers and proselytized in many previously uncharted areas. The most famous Catholic missionary to China, Matteo Ricci, came from their ranks and served there from 1583 to his death in 1610. Following Rome's official policy of focusing on creating political influence with national governments before evangelizing commoners, Ricci served in the imperial court. Garbed in flowing silk robes like a Confucian scholar, Ricci avoided teaching Christian doctrines that would be offensive in Chinese culture and even allowed converts to continue practicing ancestor worship, considering it to be more cultural than religious. This toleration for idolatry would later come back to harm the Catholic cause when the pope issued a decree in 1704 that expressly forbade ancestor worship.

Feeling betrayed, the Chinese emperor was enraged at what looked like an attempt to step on his sovereignty. He responded by severely persecuting Christians throughout China and later passing the "Edict of Expulsion and Confiscation" which forced all missionaries to either work in secular government positions or live in the foreign area of Guangzhou. From then on Catholicism went underground in China.

In God's sovereignty, the forced gathering of Catholic missionary exiles in Guangzhou led to the first Catholic translation of the New Testament in Chinese. This manuscript was given to the British Museum and later discovered by Dr. William Moseley, who spoke to many missions organizations about making a Chinese Bible.[6] After being rejected by one missions society after another, he was finally put together with Robert Morrison, the missionary who would one day complete the first ever Chinese Bible. It was this New Testament made by refugees in Guangzhou that became a major source text for his Protestant translation. How amazing it is that God would use exiled Catholic ministers to prepare the way for the ministry of the first Protestant missionary to China almost a century later. This pattern of persecution eventually leading to great spiritual fruit is a hallmark of the Chinese church to this day.

Robert Morrison taught himself Hebrew, Greek, and Latin while working in his father's workshop. In 1806 he began learning Chinese with nothing more than the British Museum's Chinese New Testament, a Chinese-Latin dictionary, and a Chinese roommate he lived with in London. Just a year later he left for China, stopping in the US on the way. Due to the laws strictly forbidding foreigners from entering the mainland at the time, Morrison lived for a short time in Guangzhou's foreign enclave and spent most of his life in Macao. Once on the field, he wasted no time and was able to complete a 1,100-page Chinese-English dictionary within nine months. It was a capital crime for Chinese to teach their native tongue to foreigners, but several risked their lives to teach Morrison and help him translate the Bible. Morrison's Chinese New Testament was completed in 1813 and relied heavily on the old Catholic translation. A year later he baptized the first recorded Protestant Chinese convert, Cai Fu. With the help of William Milne, Morrison went on to complete the Chinese Bible in 1819. After a very fruitful twenty-seven years of service to the Lord, this father of Chinese missions died in Guangzhou in 1834.

If there was ever a Chinese missionary hall of fame it would be full of names, but space limits us to just one more, perhaps the most famous of them all. Like Morrison, J. Hudson Taylor hailed from England and devoted his entire life to bringing the gospel to the Chinese. Several years before his arrival, the First Opium War had forcibly pried open China's gates to foreigners, bringing much more opportunities for mainland ministry than in Morrison's day. Taylor arrived in China at the peak of the Taiping Rebellion, a long and bloody revolt led by a man who claimed to be the brother of Jesus sent to usher in God's kingdom on earth. His writings recount the artillery bombardments of his neighborhood and the horror of watching prisoners of war brutally beheaded before his eyes.[7] All these experiences made him long even more to see China come to Christ.

What quickly set Taylor apart from the other western missionaries was his insisting on living among the Chinese and adopting native dress. This outraged many of the missionaries hiding within the walls of their mission compound. They considered his methods to be radical and even savage, forgetting that Christ too had adopted the culture of those He came to serve. Hudson Taylor's novel approach to missions, traveling upriver in junks while sporting his dyed black hair in a Chinese queue, gave him unsurpassed access to parts of inner China where no foreigner had ever trod. As the work expanded, in 1865 Taylor founded the China Inland Mission with the express purpose of sending likeminded missionaries deep into China to raise up local churches.

As the imperial government lost more ground to western powers, the empire increasingly opened up to foreign missionaries. Hospitals, orphanages, schools, and the first universities were all built by western missionaries seeking to share Christ's love through both word and deed. Many of the universities famous in China today were founded by such missionaries.

Needless to say not everyone was happy with the increasing foreign influence. With the tacit support of the Empress Dowager, the Boxer Rebellion erupted in 1898 and wreaked havoc across the nation until it was quelled by foreign armies in 1901. It was a terrifying time for missionaries as riotous hordes ransacked cities in search of foreigners and those sympathetic to them.

The Boxer Rebellion was China's last ditch effort to rid their crumbling nation of foreign influence, including their God. There are numerous tales from that era of missionary families huddled under farmhouses in silence for days before narrowly escaping with their lives. Many of those who attempted to flee south to foreign-occupied safe areas were mercilessly cut down on the roads.

Missionaries suddenly found themselves in a crucible and the China Inland Mission suffered the most. More than thirty thousand Chinese Christians and over two hundred foreign missionaries—men, women, and children—were slaughtered in the rebellion, many of them brutally hacked to death with swords and farm implements. Rightly had Morrison said many years before, "It is not possible but that this land must be watered with the blood of many martyrs before the gospel prevails generally." Much blood had been shed, but a great harvest was soon to come.

Much to the imperial palace's dismay, the defeat of the

rebels actually increased the western military presence in China. Foreign powers marched through Beijing and into the Forbidden City, many of them demanding war reparations. The Qing Dynasty was all but broken and would eventually fade into history with the child emperor's forced abdication in 1911.

Meanwhile the first decade of the twentieth century became the most fruitful for missionaries in China. By 1910 there were 5,144 Protestant missionaries in China discipling 15,500 potential native church leaders and over two hundred thousand converts.[8] The foreign missionary enterprise in China was reaching its peak.

Along with this sudden church growth came the problems frequently linked to success. Many missionary organizations felt like they needed to become more "professional" and began focusing on medical and educational reforms rather than preaching the gospel. China's physical health and prosperity became more important than her spiritual condition. In many missionary-run schools and universities the gospel became something extra only taught outside of class. As A. J. Broomhall sadly notes, "The means of presenting the gospel was replacing the gospel itself."[9] Today's gospel-less "social gospel" is definitely nothing new to the mission field.

Another problem was the virtual stranglehold that western missionaries had on their Chinese congregants. Fledgling Chinese churches were divided along western-made denominational lines and Chinese ministers were often totally dependent on their foreign mentors. The 1907 General Inter-Mission Conference clearly portrayed this western dominance. Out of the five hundred delegates who were meeting to discuss the future of Protestant Christianity in China, only six or seven were actually Chinese. It became clear that as long as the Chinese church was connected to westerners, it wouldn't keep growing and become a truly organic church.

On January 1, 1912, Sun Yat-sen, a professing Christian who had married a pastor's daughter, declared the founding of the Republic of China. Many leaders in the new government were influenced by Christianity and even made April 27, 1913 a Day of Prayer for China, requesting churches around the world to intercede on the nation's behalf. The era ended soon after Sun's death in 1924 and the republic quickly crumbled into chaos with warlords and bandits ravaging the country.

The unpredictable nature of widespread civil war made missionary work quite perilous, but those who toughed it out witnessed immense fruit in many places. Some warlords even invited them to preach to their troops and great numbers of soldiers were saved. During those violent times, many Bible institutes began all over the country where missionaries trained future Chinese church leaders. It was also during those days that Christians began worshiping in homes, the first Chinese house churches. Despite the growing anti-Christian sentiment that was being propagated by the newly-formed Chinese Communist Party, there were 8,235 Protestant missionaries on the ground in 1926.

As Communism spread, violence against Christians also increased. Communists frequently captured and executed foreign missionaries. After the Japanese invaded China in 1937, missionaries were forced to leave Japanese-occupied areas or be interned in squalid prison camps. Whether by choice or compulsion, the hostile environment created an ever-increasing stream of missionaries returning to their homelands. Leadership of the Chinese church was gradually falling into native hands.

With Mao's rise to power and the Communist takeover in 1949, the curtains finally closed on the foreign missionary effort in China. Most had been forced to leave by 1952, but Helen Willis was the last Protestant missionary to depart in 1959. As the bamboo curtain fell, to the outside world it looked like Christianity was going to once again disappear from the Middle Kingdom. God, however, had other plans.

The closing of all China's churches and imprisonment of their leaders didn't happen overnight. While Mao and his cronies tightened their grip on the people, faithful Chinese evangelists worked feverishly to bring in a harvest of souls before nightfall. Throughout the early 1950s, men like Watchman Nee planted house churches like there was no tomorrow. By 1949, Nee's "Little Flock" had grown to around seventy thousand members meeting in over 700 churches. Though he died in prison after his arrest in 1952, his writings have continued to be influential to Chinese Christians ever since.

In 1954 the Three-Self Patriotic Movement became the official government entity for handling church affairs. The organization gets its name from its emphasis on "self-governance, self-support, and self-propagation," which were interestingly all ideals originally espoused by the China Missionary Society and Hudson Taylor's China Inland Mission. During its formation, well-known Chinese pastors were asked and then coerced into joining the movement. Those who refused were usually imprisoned for decades and many died in Chinese prison labor camps. Their primary reason for refusing was their understanding that the Three-Self was ultimately under the authority of the Communist Party, not Christ. Many of them were also opposed to partnering with the leaders of the organization because they seemed to be wolves in sheep's clothing, claiming to be Christians but so theologically liberal that the unregistered church pastors doubted their salvation. Thus the underground Chinese House Church was born.

The government's extreme crackdown on all who refused to register their churches with the Three-Self put a bad taste in the mouths of many Christians that continues to this day. Although there are regions of China where Three-Self churches and house churches work together, in most areas there is a clear divide that is sometimes antagonistic.

A cloud of intense persecution formed on the horizon as Beijing tightened the noose around those refusing to go along with their religious "reforms." In the decades ahead, countless Christians would lose their homes, possessions, dignity, and even their lives because they remained faithful to their Lord and Savior.

Though tragic at the time, it was in this furnace of affliction that the Lord refined the Chinese church to form it into the unstoppable force it is today. God used an evil Communist dictator to take the foreign crutches off of Chinese Christianity so that it could become an indigenous faith. With its training wheels removed, Christianity in China exploded in ways not seen since the first century. In the flames of persecution, the dross of denominationalism brought by westerners also burned away and the Chinese church became unified in suffering. With nothing more than a scant few hidden Bibles, the Holy Spirit, and their faith in an all-mighty God, the Chinese church was being forged into a powerful weapon for God's purposes.

3

CLARIFYING THE CONFUSING

Those unfamiliar with China may think that the house churches are a secret society that meets by candlelight in caves like some mysterious Druid sect, but in actuality the Chinese House Church refers to a movement of unregistered Christian gatherings that operate independently of government authority. Far from being mysterious, these unregistered gatherings are probably more like church meetings in the Book of Acts than anything else.

Officially, the Chinese House Church as it exists today developed after Mao Zedong and the Communists came to power in 1949. China set up a government-sanctioned church called the "Three-Self Patriotic Movement" (TSPM) that is overseen by the China Christian Council (CCC). The underground (unregistered) churches in China are often called house churches because they are not allowed to congregate in official worship places like church buildings and must meet secretly in private homes and businesses.

During the days of intense persecution, leaders of unregistered church meetings were constantly on the run from the police. These traveling convicts and vagabonds began to gather followings and plant home churches. Being forced to hide together created an intense and close bond among them within short periods of time. This was the beginning of the House Church networks. These churches were literally forming in the homes of believers and were meeting without the permission or knowledge of the local government, thus they are called "underground house churches."

House churches in places like Henan Province became linked by those who traveled around preaching the gospel. Soon they became secret, but well-organized national networks with centralized leadership and local cells. The organizational structure began to be formed in the 80s and 90s under the tutelage of the founding leaders.

At first the underground Christians were just fighting to survive, but by the 90s funding and training from abroad began to come in and assist the Chinese to reach larger crowds with effective training. Bible printing, distribution, Bible schools, seminars, and even baptisms became essential parts of this underground society. This type of House Church movement became especially strong in Henan and Anhui Provinces.

One of the key components of this movement has been women. Anyone who has had exposure to the underground Chinese House Church will immediately notice that women are at the heart of it. They are often preaching, teaching, leading, administrating, and providing places to hold meetings.

Competing with this underground movement is the official church of China. After taking over the nation, the leadership within the Communist Party quickly realized that their future political success depended on their ability to control and manipulate the thoughts of the entire population, including Christians.

Though the official church in China has changed over the years, in the beginning it was implemented as a tool to register, control, and eventually eliminate Chinese Christianity. The Communist Party of China spawned the TSPM which was sold to the people as a way to remain loyal to the country and still maintain a form of godliness. The TSPM often substituted the Word of God with the propaganda of the party. Teaching from the Bible that encouraged sacrifice and devotion to the Messiah were redirected to brainwash congregants into unquestionable loyalty to the party diluting the power of the cross and the promise of Christ's return.

In its initial stages, TSPM church leaders didn't plan to assist in the destruction of Christianity in China. They were sincere and saw themselves as patriots who were standing up against enslavement and exploitation by foreign imperialists. Communist ideology was very new at the time and seemed to agree with the teachings of Jesus Christ. Communism seemed to promote equality for all, equal distribution of wealth, and community responsibility for the poor—all things that seemed to jive with Jesus' teachings.

Little did those leaders know that the atheists had planned their systematic destruction. The Christians were promised autonomy and more freedom than ever if they would join the cause of Red China. Many of them even applauded having the chains of the foreign missionary control broken off. Many of them didn't protest when the laws of an atheist government began to make rules regulating the church. Some of them began to wake up when their leaders and clergy began to be sent to labor camps for not adopting the control mechanisms of the government at a faster pace. By the time that the church realized what was going on and began to resist, it was too late.

The TSPM was created not only as a control mechanism to register, monitor, and redirect the teachings of the Christian church, but it was also meant to wean the church off of the Truth. According to China News and Church Report there are seven very strict rules to be followed in Three-Self Churches:

1. Christian believers must fervently love the People's Republic of China, support the leadership of the Chinese Communist Party and the Peoples' Government, uphold the unification of the motherland and the harmony among ethnic groups, and work steadfastly on the road of socialism.

2. Christian believers must strictly abide by all the laws, regulations, and policies of the Communist Party and the State and strive to be patriotic and law abiding citizens.

3. Christian believers must actively work to increase the material wealth and cultivate the spiritual morals of the socialist civilization. They must comply with the government's labor codes and strive to contribute to the development of the "Four Modernizations" established by the Communist Party. When scheduled religious activities are in conflict with production and work schedules, the economic activities must take priority.

4. A permit must be obtained from the county State Administration for Religious Affairs in order to establish religious meeting points. No unauthorized meeting points are allowed.

5. Christian believers must actively cooperate with the government to thoroughly carry out the party's religious policies to the letter. They shall not persuade and force others to believe in Christianity. They shall not brainwash teenagers under 18 with religious beliefs. They shall not bring children under 18 to religious activities.

6. One should see a doctor for medication when sick. Christian

believers must not resort to prayer alone for healing so as not to endanger people's health and lives.

7. Christian believers shall not preach their religion outside the church building and specific places which have been designated for religious activities. They shall not preach itinerantly. They shall not receive self-proclaimed evangelists into their homes, churches or meeting points. [10]

In addition to these seven rules are codes that are enforced, but not necessarily written in legislation, which is a common practice in China. These codes prevent evangelism, children's ministry, preaching by visiting pastors, unauthorized baptism, unauthorized independent Bible training, multinational cooperation, printing teaching materials, handing out Bibles, teaching about the Virgin Birth, the Second Coming, or the Resurrection.

Anyone who has ever had to go through immigration, start a business, or watch a court procedure in China quickly learns that there are few written rules that are actually practiced in China. Most of the rules are widely understood, but rarely captured on paper.

In China, there is a lot of bureaucracy and the names and titles that we do not have in the West can cause confusion. The following chart of the chain of command in China can make things a bit easier to understand.

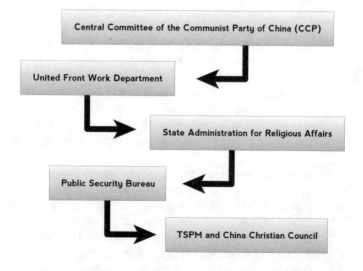

The Communist Party is at the top of the chain and by definition, one must be a professed atheist to be a part of the Communist Party. The atheists in the Communist Party dictate the religious policy to then be written up by the United Front Department. The laws that are written on the books by the United Front are then carried out by the State Administration for Religious Affairs. This Bureau also writes the rules regarding religion and foreigners.

The China Christian Council and the Three-Self Patriotic Movement are the bodies that both fall under the State Administration for Religious Affairs. These two bodies have the impossible task of keeping the church members under control, compliant with policy, and spiritually satisfied. At the same time they must always be putting forth the best possible presentation for foreigners.

This system is similar in many ways to what Jeroboam set up in the Old Testament in the final days of Israel. After Israel and Judah were divided, many Israelites were brokenhearted. The pain was eased for many during the annual pilgrimages to the Temple in Jerusalem which was in the territory of Judah. Jerusalem was rich in history and held deep meaning for the Jews, and those who traveled from the land of Israel were emotionally attached to Rehoboam's capital city.

To curb this challenge to Israeli patriotism, King Jeroboam built new places of worship. He fired all of the priests of the Lord and installed new priests. In like manner, to curb the challenge to Chinese patriotism, the Chinese formed their own church and chose their own leaders.

Many of the unauthorized Christian leaders were hunted down, publicly humiliated, beaten, jailed and had their families stripped of everything and ostracized from the community. Many of them were given the opportunity to deny Christ, swear their allegiance to the Communist Party, and avoid all of the hardships and pain. There were many reports of those who denied Christ being rewarded with leadership in the official TSPM church.

Those that denied Christ were placed in high positions in the official church and those that didn't went on the run from the authorities, becoming leaders in the underground movement. This created a huge divide between the underground church and the official church in China, a divide that exists to this day.

Many official church members were also used by the government to secretly infiltrate underground House Church meetings, identify the locations, leaders, and networks, record details and then turn them in. This of course led to distrust and deeply-buried animosity.

Because of the betrayal that many believers felt from the first leaders of the official church in China, there remains a deep scar that is still raw and sensitive. Although the situation between the House Church and the Three-Self has improved in many parts of China, that scar in particular continues to keep the House Church from registering with the government.

What is the main difference between the Three-Self Church and the House Church in China today? It would be best to get the answer to this question directly from Chinese who are still living in their homeland. In our previous publication, *The Heavenly People*, interviews were conducted with senior members of the underground House Church networks in Henan and Anhui Province. The following is a reprint of those interviews:

This interview was with a senior leader who is from a House Church network in Henan Province and has been charged with caring for churches in Guangdong, Guangxi, Yunnan, Guizhou, and overseeing missionaries sent to South East Asia. It took place in a car driving from parking place to parking place in Humen, China on April 14, 2009.

In America and Europe there are many people claiming that there is growing religious freedom in China. Is this true?

Yes and no. China is a big country and there have been many changes, but some of those changes have only been new ways of expressing old habits.

Can you elaborate? Many people in West feel that there is freedom for Christians in China and they cannot understand why the house churches will not register with the government.

This topic is very important to me. I have never discussed this with any foreigner before. We believe that

Christians should not get political. We don't want to argue with anyone, we don't want to get involved in politics. We don't want to be for China what the Roman Catholic Church was in western history, but we also do not want to have the politicians running the church, setting the doctrine, and leading us away from Christ.

The government in China controls the Three-Self Church and has led many people away from the truth. In 1983, when I was living in my hometown in southern Henan Province, there was a surge of persecution of Christians in China. The government was not able to destroy the church under Mao Zedong, so they tried a different tactic under Deng Xiaoping: control. Many pastors were arrested. During that time my older sister who was a well-known leader in our hometown was arrested and told to deny Christ. If she would deny Jesus Christ, they promised she would be released from prison and be given a post in the official church. The first leaders of the Three-Self Church in my area were all people who had denied Jesus Christ. My sister served three years in prison for refusing to deny the name of Jesus Christ.

Many pastors in the Three-Self Church in China are paid by the government. They are salaried employees. This is not true everywhere of course, but it is true in my hometown (Henan). If pastors are paid by an Atheistic government, who is their real boss?

For those who do not believe what we are saying, let them see for themselves. They can look into it and find that the government decides who is ordained. The government decides who a church's pastor is. The government dictates the amount of baptisms allowed per month or year. The government dictates how many Bibles can be distributed. The government dictates what can be taught or not taught in the churches. The government dictates where a pastor can preach and not preach. These are all facts that can be proven. They cannot be denied.

The Bible clearly says that we are one body. We are the Body of Christ. How can we be separated? How can the government tell us that churches in Guiyang cannot fellowship with churches in Kashgar? How can the government tell us that westerners cannot fellowship with believers in Nanyang? How can the government tell us that Chinese cannot attend international services in Kunming without a foreign passport? The Body of Christ is one body. It cannot be separated.

You mentioned before that the government controls what is taught in the Three-Self Churches of China. How do you know this? You are a part of the underground House Church movement. Do you have any proof of these teachings?

Yes. Have you ever been to a Three-Self Church?

No. I have attempted a few times in Kunming a couple of years ago, but because I was a foreigner I was denied entrance every time.

Inside the official government churches there are red banners stretched from one side of the room to the other. They are one of the most prominent displays in the churches and are put up by the *Ai Guo* or "love country" movement, also known as the patriotic movement, that reminds all believers that country comes before God. Under those banners is a posting of laws. There are 18 sections or parts on these postings. Some postings have fewer sections and some churches have taken them down all together, but they are still very much a part of the government church of China. Among those postings the patrons are told that they cannot baptize people under the age of eighteen, they cannot teach about the resurrection of Jesus Christ and they can't teach about the Second Coming.

Are these still posted at the front of the churches today in 2009 though?

Oh yes, they are and I can take a picture of them for you and get it to you if you want.

An interview with another leader from a different network in Anhui Province is provided here in order to give a different opinion and broader perspective. This interview was done with the head pastor of a network of about one million believers in Anhui on April 9, 2009.

In America and Europe there are many people claiming that there is growing religious freedom in China. Is this true?

I would agree that there is more religious freedom today than before in most areas.

Are there restrictions on Christians in China? If so, what are they?

Yes. There are many freedoms that we still do not have in China. I know that this is hard for the church in the West to understand. We (the house churches in Anhui) do not have, nor are we allowed to have, an outlet to let the world know the things that we face on a daily basis. The basic tenets of our faith such as fellowship, evangelism, teaching children about Christian values—these are all forbidden in China.

There have been Christian leaders and pastors from America and Europe who have been asked to come and see the practice of Christianity in China. They have seen the difference and have even been asked to come and speak at many venues (including churches). During these speaking engagements they have not been told what to speak about or what not to speak about. The number of people present during these events has been amazing. After they return back to their home countries they tell others about the freedoms in China. What is your response to this?

Oh, this is a common practice of the Chinese Government. Of course these foreigners see these things. It is a show that has been arranged by the government. If they believe what they see during this time then they are believing a lie.

Do you want proof? Tell those leaders who say this after a trip to China that they should arrange another trip to China, but this time they can tell the government that they do not need their help. They can arrange their own trip, their own speaking engagements, and they can kindly decline the involvement of the government. Then we will see how things go. Only those who want the truth will do this. Others who continue to repeat what the government has given them are willfully believing a lie.

There are many well-known workers in China who are trying to unite the house churches with the government in China in an arrangement similar to the Three-Self Church in China. How do you feel about this?

With the work that we do, it is not possible for me to register.

Why?

You see, one of the big problems is that the head of any government church in China would be run by an atheist. Someone who does not believe in what the Word of God says would be telling us how to practice it. Maybe this is something that others can compromise, but I believe that the Word of God is clear: I must preach the Word, I must reach the lost, I must pray for the sick—these are the things that I must do.

Even if I were to register—where would I register? Any city where I register would be on my license and I would not be able to conduct the work that I do today. I would not be able to travel to other areas and evangelize as I do today all over China. I have been called to preach the Word in many areas of China, how can I agree to stay in just one city?

Many leaders and experts in the West claim that there are enough Bibles in China. What is your response to them?

There are not enough Bibles in China.

Why is that? Is that because the government makes it hard to get them or because the areas that are in need are too poor to purchase their own Bibles?

Both. Right now, almost all of our work is in the villages. The people who live in these areas are not able to afford Bibles, but this is not the only reason. We are not able to get access to the number of Bibles that we need.

Many people in the West quote from Amity Press that there are more than enough Bibles made in China. Do you know that more Bibles are made in China than anywhere else in the world?

Listen, when I go to the Three-Self church in Hefei to purchase Bibles I can buy maybe 5 or 10 without any problem. However, if I purchase large numbers of Bibles or put in a request for numbers exceeding a thousand or so, I am asked why I need so many, where they are going, who they are going to, etc. My information is logged and kept on record for large purchases. This is not safe for me, so I get my Bibles from an underground press.

But do you know—even with the ability to purchase Bibles—there are not enough. Even through the official channels.

Are you saying that there are not enough Bibles available through the Three-Self Church?

Yes, I am saying that there are not enough Bibles through the official churches. There have been many times when I went to Hefei Three-Self church to buy only between 5 and 10 Bibles and was turned away because they didn't have any. When the meetings take place to distribute Bibles from the printing office to the Three-Self Churches many negotiations take place. For instance, one church leader might say, "We need one million Bibles." The response from the government official in return might be, "Why do you need so many? You don't need that many. You will only get 200,000." And that is that. End of story. [11]

4

TESTED BY FIRE

At Los Angeles' Cottonwood Christian Center in 2010, Brother Ren—the man partially responsible for that intrepid airlift of Bibles mentioned earlier—introduced his dear friend Brother Yun to a packed house. The crowd had gathered to hear from this man who had endured great persecution and miraculously escaped from a Chinese maximum security prison. It was a special privilege that night to also have Peter Xu, the founder of China's Born Again Movement, on stage as well. Before giving the floor to Yun, Ren gave some background on China's spiritual situation after the Communist takeover.

"In 1949 the Communist Party came to power in China," he began. "As a first order of business, the Communist Party began to wipe the country clean of any visible signs of Christianity. Pastors and evangelists were tortured, killed, or sent to labor camps where they would suffer, rot and die. Bibles and hymnals were piled up in public squares and burned. Missionaries were kicked out of the country. Churches were closed, never to be opened up again. The world watched as China purged itself of Christians and all signs of Christianity."

The former Beijing bureau chief for *Time* Magazine and respected authority on China wrote in his landmark book, *Jesus in Beijing,* "Many former missionaries from the West cried when they saw all of their dedication and sacrifice washed away. The world waited for the first glimpse back into the country to see if there were any Christians left. When the doors to China finally did open, Mao Zedong's Wife Jiang Qing was quoted as boasting to the foreign delegation that "Christianity in China has been confined to the history section of the museum. It is dead and buried."[12]

Mao Zedong stood in front of the Tiananmen Square audience on October 1, 1949 and announced a new era for China.

The first order of business was to ensure a one way exit for all foreign missionaries. Next he would work on eradicating the faith from the native population. However, we will see that the impact of his actions could not have been more counterproductive. Romans 8:28 really rings true when we see how God worked out the foolish schemes of evil men to expand His church. By effectively removing the foreign community from China, the Communist government was paving the way for a more powerful revival than had ever been recorded in Chinese history. Although the 1950s and 60s saw many pastors and Christian leaders sent to gulags where they were indoctrinated, tortured, or killed, a great spiritual harvest would follow.

One of the largest attempts at eradicating Christianity from the borders of China was attempted during the Great Leap Forward (1958-1961). Perhaps it is more than a coincidence that the worst famine, poverty, and anguish ever recorded in Chinese history all took place during this intense time of Christian persecution. Just like under the Romans in the first century, believers were scattered to the winds because of the persecution. As in the past, when those believers were scattered they took their zeal and faith in Jesus with them and shared the Good News in areas that might never have heard it otherwise.

In order to purge China of Christianity, it was important to proceed in phases because many Chinese Christians believed they were also doing what was best for their country. They gathered well-known Christian leaders and tried to get them to follow the Party line, knowing full well that if the shepherds were on board the sheep would soon follow. Once all of the believers were registered and put in controlled areas, mass indoctrination programs could be implemented and the leadership could be disposed of. This would ensure the further consolidation of the Party's power.

Mao held the same view as Marx and Lenin—quite fitting, considering that Russia paid to put him in power and saved him from annihilation by the Nationalists on numerous occasions. He believed that religion was the "opiate of the masses" and should be eliminated by internal struggle. Y.T. Wu (Wu Yaozong) published the "Christian Manifesto" at the prompting of the Communist Party and by 1952 more than four hundred thousand Chinese Christians had signed it. The manifesto stated that Christianity was essentially a mechanism of western imperialism and Chinese Christians should be self-reliant and separate themselves from all western instruction. Even though he unwittingly helped disassemble the Chinese church, the Communist government that he assisted eventually turned on him as well and sent him to labor camp for "re-education" during the Cultural Revolution.

In those days enthusiastic students went throughout China seeking out "class enemies," a term not specifically defined but understood to mean anyone who did not agree with everything taught by the Communist Party. Christians were considered some of the foremost class enemies. Those who did not immediately renounce their faith were dragged out to be tried in make-shift courts, publicly humiliated and persecuted. They were often forced to wear dunce caps or carry signs that advertised their alleged crimes against the state. A common phrase on the dunce cap of a Christian was, "Down with the foul intellectual" because many Christians in China at that time had been exposed to western education and were considered to be worthless intellectuals. As enemies of the state (including women and children) were paraded down the street wearing these dunce caps, it was the civic duty of locals to verbally and physically abuse them.

Mai Fu Ren was a Christian living in Shantou when Mao came to power. His mother and father were Christians and wanted him to be a missionary. The author met him while the book *Project Pearl* was about to go to print. The book told the amazing story of a former US Marine who led a daring operation to smuggle one million Bibles into Shantou, China in 1981. The author was in Shantou meeting with House Church leaders to discuss the need for Chinese believers to put their lives on the line in the same way in order to get God's Word into North Korea when he ran into Mai Fu Ren. On the same beach where the massive Bible delivery had taken place, a man in his eighties came up to the author and spoke to him in perfect English. When asked if he had ever heard about the one million Bibles dropped on those shores in 1981 he smiled and replied, "Heard about it? Son, I was there!" and began to explain how he had buried Bibles in the sand to hide them from the authorities and dug them up days later to pack them on to delivery vehicles.

Mai Fu Ren remembered when the Communists took power in China in 1949. His family had become enemies of the state overnight because his father was a pastor and worked closely with foreign missionaries. His family members were soon arrested and scattered throughout Guangdong Province to serve in intense re-education camps. Both of his parents were sent to labor camps where they were forced to work until they succumbed to premature death. Many of Mai Fu Ren's twelve brothers and sisters died in those camps as well.

"The police pointed at me and yelled, 'You are an anti-revolutionary!" Mai Fu Ren recounted. "They announced over the loud speakers, 'Mai Fu Ren is an anti-revolutionary!'" For delivering Bibles in China, Mai Fu Ren spent a total of thirty years in prison.

Though his suffering and loss were extreme, they were not unique for the Chinese in those days. Christians throughout China were experiencing the same kind of difficult challenges, torture, and even death for refusing to deny the name of Jesus Christ. The Chinese government employed a united front against not only the Christian faithful, but anyone Mao's regime was suspicious of.

In her book, *Mao, The Unknown Story*, Jung Chang and her historian husband Jon Holliday record the results of a decade of research on Mao. They begin the biography by writing, "Mao Tse-Tung, who for decades held absolute power over the lives of one-quarter of the world's population, was responsible for well over seventy million deaths in peacetime, more than any other twentieth-century leader." Seventy million is not an easy number to fathom. Put into perspective, it is almost the same as killing the entire populations of Sweden, Finland, Norway, Denmark and the Netherlands...twice. There aren't any museums, federal holidays, or even a simple monument built to remember these millions of poor souls.

Soon after the rise of the Communist Party in China, Mao's personality cult swept the nation. Implementing the personality cult of Chairman Mao was vital to consolidating the power that was being wielded against the personal lives of so many citizens.

Benjamin, of whom we'll learn more about later, is a well-known Christian singer in China. During a meeting in Malaysia he shared the memories he had of being a small boy during that time. He vividly remembered the personality cult that was put into place shortly after Mao had come to power.

"I can remember when a member of our family was cleaning the portrait of Mao. He wanted to honor the picture of Mao by keeping it perfectly clean even though the rest of his home was dirty and poor. He didn't have any proper cleaning detergent, so he heated up water and used it to clean his portrait. However, the water and his rag were so hot that the steam ruined the paint on Mao's cheek. The paint came right off of the portrait! The man panicked. He did not have the money to buy a new one and could not afford to have the town see what he had done. It was a horrible mistake. Other relatives quickly came and publicly condemned him. Destroying a picture of Mao Zedong was a punishable offense."

Personality cults in totalitarian regimes that attempt to radically transform society are not uncommon, but there were characteristics unique to the worship of Mao. Mao was the face of the struggles of the revolution. China, by its very nature, is more paternal than most countries.

Below is a poster from 1954 that says, "Chairman Mao gives us a happy life." Every home was required to have a picture of Chairman Mao, usually an oil painting, and it was to remain clean enough to be ready for inspection.

History books would have us believe that Mao and his army forced the country to bow to his power, but that is not exactly true.

IISH / Stefan R. Landsberger Collections, chineseposters.net

At that time China had just been humiliated by the Japanese. A group of islands off the east coast of China had been able to subjugate a large portion of the most populated country in the world with a handful of disciplined troops. Japanese occupation was just the culmination of decades of foreign domination in China. Places like Shanghai, Beijing, Qingdao, and Hong Kong had long been under western control before the Japanese took them. The Chinese felt helpless against these powers and demoralized that such small armies could infringe on their soil with little effort. The Chinese were looking for a hero who could restore honor and dignity to the nation. Rather than rejecting Chairman Mao, many actually welcomed him. They were infatuated by him, praised his name, and deified everything he did. Army leaders and spiritual leaders followed the energy of the mobs.

Even the Dalai Lama played into this mania. There is a handwritten letter written from the Dalai Lama in a Buddhist temple in Beijing that "Free Tibet" activists and the Dalai Lama would like to forget. In it the Dalai Lama wrote words of praise that come close to deifying Mao. A portion of it reads:

> Oh, the Triratna (Buddha, Dharma and Sangha), which bestow blessings on the world. Protect us with your incomparable and blessed light which shines forever.
> O! Chairman Mao! Your brilliance and deeds are like those of Brahma and Mahasammata, creators of the world. Only from an infinite number of good deeds can such a leader be born, who is like the sun shining over the world. Your writings are precious like pearls, abundant and powerful as the high tide of the ocean reaching the edges of the sky. O! most honourable Chairman Mao, may you long live. All people look to you as to a kind protecting mother, they paint pictures of you with hearts full of emotion. May you live in the world forever and point out to us the peaceful road. Our vast land was burdened with pain, with shackles and darkness. You liberated all with your brilliance. People now are happy, full of blessing![13]

This hymn shows that at one time even the leader of Buddhists worldwide bowed to Mao. Such infatuation was enrapturing everyone in China. Everything, that is, except the Christians. A determination to worship God over man was why Christians like Mai Fu Ren and his family were such a threat to the government and its Maoist cult. They held on to the truth of Jesus Christ and did not bow to the newly-proclaimed savior of China.

The Dalai Lama was not the only one to compare Chairman Mao to the sun, nor was he the first, but he was one of the top religious leaders in China that gave his endorsement of the personality cult mania.

Below is a poster that could be found in China during Mao's day that makes him out to be the sun shining light on all the people. Even in China today it's not uncommon to see shiny gold cards with Chairman Mao's image on them hanging from the rear view mirrors of taxis. The shiny gold material is designed to symbolize sun-like radiance.

IISH / Stefan R. Landsberger Collections, chineseposters.net

One day while traveling from Shenzhen to Guangzhou by taxi, the author saw the Chairman Mao image hanging from the mirror. The half-balding image of the beloved and long-dead leader staring at the passengers was quite creepy. A conversation ensued. When facetiously asked who it was a picture of, the driver replied with complete surprise, "You don't know who that is? That is Chairman Mao, the founder of our country. How do you not know who that is?"

"I am from America. We never learned about Chairman Mao in American school. Why do you have a picture of him in your car?"

His eyes glanced back at the strange foreign passenger. "He was a great leader of China and even now he is able to provide my car with protection from disasters and bring me good luck."

"Well don't you think he should be turned around so that he can see the road? I think he would be able to help us avoid disaster if he actually watched where he was going." Such humor was totally lost on the driver.

During the Cultural Revolution, the cult of Mao not only had its savior, but like Christianity it even had a holy book.

毛主席万岁！万万岁！

IISH / Stefan R. Landsberger Collections, chineseposters.net

All over China posters like this showed every citizen carrying a copy of *Quotations from Chairman Mao Tse-Tung*, known diminutively in the West as "*The Little Red Book*." Everywhere the Chinese traveled, they were to have this book in hand. Second to only the Holy Bible, Mao's *Little Red Book* is the next most printed book in history. It also holds the world record for being the most printed book in less than four years with 720 million copies in print by the end of 1967. The personality cult with its red booklet and constant brainwashing all eventually led to complete governmental control of everything and certain destruction for anyone who was willing to oppose worship of the Chairman.

At the same time, Mao also implemented many practical things that greatly assisted the spread of the gospel. Even in his days of intense hatred for the Christian community, he unwittingly helped proselytization in ways that were never even imaginable before his time. He united in one country a diverse land that included Tibet and Xinjiang—areas that had previously been independent nations—which effectively eliminated the need for passports and travel documents in order for secret missionaries to serve in those areas. He connected the entire country with railways and road systems that helped make the hardest to reach places much more accessible to Christ's ambassadors.

Another huge work he accomplished was uniting the entire country under a single language. Before learning Mandarin Chinese was compulsory in China, hundreds of minority languages made it impossible for someone to preach in many different areas without learning each region's language. Thanks to Mao, it became possible to share the gospel, conduct training, and implement mass Bible printing in one language for all of China. If that wasn't enough, he even ordered the Chinese characters to be simplified so more people could learn to read and write, effectively opening the door for millions of people to read the Bible.

Ironically, Mao's pragmatic approach to making his country more mobile, literate, and competitive would defeat his other goal of destroying Christianity in China. Even police pursuit of preachers served to extend the Kingdom of God. Being on the run forced the evangelists to travel great distances around the country as itinerate preachers, resulting in even more areas hearing about Christ than if the police hadn't been making them flee. It is safe to say that few people in the history of China did more for facilitating the spread of the Good News than Chairman Mao.

One of several men well-known for not bowing to Chairman Mao was Lin Xianggao, better known as Samuel Lamb. Although his attacks on Brother Yun (whom he has never met) and Yun's testimony, *The Heavenly Man* (which he has never read), have caused some controversy, he remains an example of diehard Christian faith against all odds. Though he has some disagreements with many in the Back to Jerusalem Movement, he is undoubtedly a true man of God who has dedicated his life to serving the Lord.

Samuel Lamb was born among the Portuguese in Macau and raised among the British in Hong Kong. After Mao came to power, more than one hundred thousand Chinese fled to Hong Kong every month. By 1955, there were more than 2.2 million people living in Hong Kong, turning it into one of the most densely populated cities in the world. Most Christians who had the chance to leave China in the 1950s, 60s, and 70s did, but not Lamb. He could have easily resided in Hong Kong and ministered to the mass influx of Chinese refugees, started a nice church, and even settled down with his family. Instead, Samuel Lamb answered God's call and served inside China during the most terrifying days of her history.

He refused to bow to the new god of China and was labeled as a counter-revolutionary, arrested, and thrown into prison. After more than a year in prison he was released and told that he should never teach the Word of God again. However, it was not long before he was pastoring a church again in Guangzhou. When he was arrested again in 1958, he was given a twenty-year sentence and put to work on a farm out of sight and mind. Things changed when he was caught making a handwritten copy of the Bible. The authorities realized they had found a man that could not be beaten down, so they sent him to a coal mine for twenty years of hard labor.

He got through many winters without proper clothing and many summers without air conditioning. People were dying all around him from beatings, work accidents, and frostbite, but by God's grace he survived. The suffering didn't end when he was finally released after twenty years. He returned home to be greeted with the news of the death of his wife and father. His mother was also very ill and died soon after his return.

Instead of finding a way to escape China to find a better life in Hong Kong or abroad, he began to preach the gospel again. His church grew larger than it was before his imprisonment. The Chinese government was not able to stop the Word from going forth.

Samuel Lamb's humble church of five thousand now meets in small rooms in Guangzhou where everyone crowds together to hear him preach through a series of CCTV cameras and monitors. Though he is constantly being harassed and even detained from time to time, the authorities have left him alone for the most part, probably because they have bigger problems in the north. His church is but a small sampling of the tens of millions of believers scattered throughout China's House Church networks.

The persecution in China led many believers to preach the Good News "on the go" which created a huge logistical problem for the Public Security Bureau. Instead of a church like Pastor Lamb's where the congregation meets regularly in the same location, churches began blossoming in the rural areas all over Henan, Anhui, and Shandong. The PSB used to think that pastors like Lamb posed huge threats to their vision for a New China, but in their minds churches like the one led by Pastor Lamb were from the good old days. Such stationary churches took few resources to monitor and the pastor could easily be summoned to the local police station for questioning at any time. However, this new breed of pastors was running throughout the countryside, escaping the police and infecting every location they travelled to with their teachings about Christ. Instead of a few thousand people in a contained environment, now the police had to deal with several million spread over a vast area.

5

FROM GOOSE FECES TO GULAGS:
THE FOUNDING OF CHINA GOSPEL FELLOWSHIP

To keep this book from turning into a collection of mere facts and historical data, great efforts have been made to include the firsthand accounts of Chinese House Church believers whenever possible. There is no better way to understand the experiences of Chinese Christians than to relive them in the mind's eye through testimonies of eyewitnesses. There is also no more fitting testimony to start with than that of a founding member of the largest House Church network in China. The next two chapters contain Pastor Shen Xiaoming's personal account of growing up under Mao, witnessing massive revival in Henan Province, and seeing the formation of the China Gospel Fellowship. [14]

> Shen Xiaoming: On December 10, 1957, I was born in a southern village of Henan Province. Those were times when government reports of agricultural abundance were empty and false. According to the Communist Party, each acre of land could yield many thousands of pounds of crops, even tens of thousands, but in reality the land yielded nothing and the people of China were starving. Everyone showed signs of malnutrition.
>
> Tens of thousands of people died in the Mao-made disaster. In the village where I lived, all the tree bark had been consumed. One day my mother used all our money to buy a few pounds of tree bark so she could make soup for us to stay alive. Unfortunately we were poisoned from that tree bark and it made everyone extremely sick. My mother wept throughout the night, certain that she would die and leave her children behind. My father and grandparents

had already passed away and there was no one to take care of us.

I was only three or four years old and remember very little, but one thing I cannot forget is the taste of goose excrement. We would have to search around the areas where the geese defecated so that we could have something to eat.

Those years were hard for everyone. I was called the "cat with nine lives" because most of the children in my village had already died, but I somehow managed to survive. My mother and I were the only ones who remained alive in our family. As a result I became very close to her.

During those days everyone was required to go out and work in food distribution. My mother had to go and work as well. She would leave early in the morning and return late at night. She would lock me up in the house to prevent me from leaving. I missed her so much during that time that I would often fall asleep crying at the door waiting for her.

My mother soon remarried and as the family grew, I found myself as more of an outsider. I had a horrible relationship with my step-father. From that relationship with my step-father and step-family I began to develop hatred toward everyone around me.

Not long after I started primary school, the Cultural Revolution began. Every day we witnessed criticism sessions where peers would condemn counter-revolutionaries. I remember an occasion when a group of people who believed in Jesus was paraded through the streets wearing tall hats with paper labels stuck to their clothes. A huge crowd followed behind cursing and swearing at them. I too followed, but did not dare make a sound, because my uncle's family was Christian. When I was young, my maternal grandmother named me "Victor" because her hope was that I would grow up to be a victorious Christian. Even though I had many years of education in atheism and evolution, my deep feelings for Christians like my grandmother and uncle never faded.

In 1975, toward the end of the Cultural Revolution, as I was graduating from High School I contracted rheumatoid arthritis, which was difficult to treat and caused me great pain. Our family was very poor and we were unable to seek medical treatment. I often wrestled with thoughts of killing myself. Each day was filled with tears, as I bitterly hated myself for having been dealt such a bitter fate. My days were soon occupied with questions of what methods I could use to commit suicide.

Soon things turned even worse. In 1978, my mother suddenly fell ill. The doctors diagnosed her with cancer. We tried to borrow money from everyone we knew for her medical treatment. By August 1979, we had spent everything. Eventually, she couldn't walk or even swallow food. All she could do was wait for death. Mother told me that her last wish was to visit my uncle, so that she might bid her final farewell to her relatives there. She asked me if I would accompany her. Thinking that mother would die very soon, and knowing that I too had no desire to live any longer, I agreed to join her in saying our last goodbyes.

We were a pitiful sight as my mother and I rode on a rickshaw and then had to both be carried into my uncle's house. At once my uncle's family began to cry and immediately shared the gospel with us. After they finished sharing the gospel with us, my mother accepted Jesus. I was hesitant and skeptical, but had nothing to lose.

Suddenly something miraculous took place. I can't explain it, but my mother was able to eat again. At that time, I thought it was just a momentary reaction out of her excitement or maybe a mere psychological phenomenon. However, the second day passed, and then the third and it was confirmed that my mother was completely healed! After that day, my mother never again took her medication. She was completely healed and I had seen it with my own eyes. It was clear that this was real, but no one was able to explain it to me.

One day I was able to borrow a radio from my aunt's house and listened to a Christian radio broadcast from Hong Kong called, "Good Friend Station" that told stories about Jesus. I began to listen every night from six in the evening until after midnight and I kept notes on everything that they taught. In this way I was able to learn that Jesus is the Son of God and how He was crucified for our sins, was resurrected, and gave us new life. At that time I truly received Jesus as my Lord and Savior.

After receiving Jesus I was given a new life, a life without fear and hurt. Many of the villagers heard about my conversion and they also rejoiced. They brought their unbelieving sons and daughters to my house and asked me to share the gospel with them. The Holy Spirit began to move mightily and people were added to the church every day.

In the summer of 1980 the House Church in our village was formally established. Initially we only had a few people who were teenagers, but by 1982 we had close to 200 people. There were many questions for me to answer, but no way for me to learn more until one day an older lady came by my house when I was praying in the garden. The lady told me that she was a Christian teacher from Xi'an. She told me that I could write to a group in Hong Kong and ask for a Bible. I knew that it was risky but I did it anyway. A few months later, they sent me one!

Tears rolled down my face as I held that copy of the Bible in my hands. Christians from all around heard that I had a Bible and traveled for miles to come and see it. From then on we kept on copying every chapter and verse by hand and distributing the copies. The gospel began to spread like wild fire. Revival broke out, the sick were healed, and even the dead were raised. The social impact from the spreading of the gospel was also great. Children respected their parents, parents loved their children, crime rates went down, etc., but things took a dramatic turn in the spring of 1982 when the party officials came to our church and declared our Christian meetings illegal. We were given a stack of papers from the government to study them carefully. The contents of those documents shocked us when we read about the "15 Prohibitions." These 15 statutes were contrary to the Word of God and impossible for us to follow.

On Christmas Day, 1982, there were more than 300 of us celebrating and praying when all of a sudden the county officials arrived and surrounded us. I was arrested and was their prime target. I had to endure a barrage of verbal attacks for about two to three hours. I began to cry out to the Lord, "Oh Lord, how can you allow these men to take your name in vain?" Suddenly the leader of the interrogation calmed down. He said nothing else and left the room.

After that arrest it was clear that we would have to meet in secret. Even when we took our meetings underground, the church grew faster than ever before.

On July 9th, 1983, there was a nationwide crackdown on the House Church and I was one of their number one targets. The police went to my house looking for me. They interrogated my step-father who was not a Christian and told the police about all the possible places I might be. I remained on the run. Life on the run was challenging but full of miracles.

At the end of 1984 we had established more than 200 host families. Each time we had a meeting we saw gatherings of people in the hundreds. Everywhere we went, entire villages would swarm the meeting places. From those meetings, evangelists were sent out to preach the gospel in the surrounding cities and towns. Within two years we saw more than 30,000 people come to the Lord. Consequently, my name was also in the hands of the Security Bureau. I was traveling all the time and preaching. One time I arrived in a village and there were many believers so I asked them, "Who preached the gospel to you?" and they replied, "You did." I told them that they must be kidding I was sure I had never been to their village before, but they assured me that this was indeed the case and that they had the tape recordings to prove it.. They told me that one month after I had preached to them they saw 25 churches established.

As evangelists, we constantly reminded each other that we must always be ready to go to jail. I even kept my hair short so that the police would not have anything to grab on to when I ran. I would also loosen all the buttons on my shirt before starting a meeting. I did this for the first ten years of ministry. Many of us evangelists would go many days without a shower. Our clothes became our blankets at night. We often slept in open fields or cow sheds. Many of us had gnats on our bodies and when we would get bored we would pick them off of each other.

One day while we were conducting a meeting, Public Security Bureau officials came and sealed off all exits to the house that I was preaching in. I and more than 90 members who were at the meeting were promptly taken away to the local police station. I was locked up for a night in a cell with a floor area of four square meters. The next day, they interrogated and tortured me, and were ready to transfer another brother and myself to the county prison. The rest of our members were fined and then released.

There was a chief of the Public Security Bureau who learned of my arrest and could not control his elation. He personally drove to see me and to escort me to prison. On the way, he told me with delight, "It took me so many years to find you. This time, there will be no turning back. You will surely die in Xidagang (the detention prison)."

As I entered the prison, I saw a large group of men who were jaundiced and scrawny-looking prisoners, each bare-bodied and wearing only a pair of shorts. Their shorts were often worn out and you could see their bottoms through the holes. The whole scene was a scary sight.

In prison I didn't have a Bible. All I could do was to meditate on the verses I remembered and silently pray to God for strength to overcome amidst suffering. God answered my prayer for strength. I never desired an early release from prison. When such thoughts surfaced, I immediately prayed for God to strengthen and give me resolve. After only three months I was released. The police chief's prediction that I would die in prison went unfulfilled.

As I began to minister again, I could see the Body of Christ growing. House meetings developed into local churches. Brothers and sisters who were forced to leave their homes repeatedly formed alliances with one another. We began to refer to these alliances as "united missions." At that time I remember a brother saying, "All of us walk the same path. We are a gospel fellowship." Thus our network accrued the label "Gospel Fellowship" or "China Gospel

Fellowship." This became a term that was widely used. The area that we are from in Henan is called Tanghe. Tanghe is the largest county in Henan Province and later became synonymous with the China Gospel Fellowship. One of the highly-respected founders of Tanghe Fellowship from the earliest years is a man named Uncle Fang.

In the spring of 1994 we saw a true increase in our evangelistic mission. We gathered in Tanghe and prayed over seventy evangelists who were sent out to more than twenty different provinces. A year later the results were astounding! The gospel was preached, churches were established, our network had expanded, and our understanding grew. For instance, there were two young sisters whose names were Xile and Xiazhe who went to Inner Mongolia. Their combined age was barely forty years. They had planted churches containing thousands of families in only a year. When they were preparing to return home many of the converts did not want them to leave so they followed them for several thousand miles on their journey home to Tanghe.

I left my home in 1983 was out preaching the gospel until 1994, never even entertaining thoughts about marriage. One day I stopped to pray to the Lord about a future wife. I asked him to prepare a wife for me according to His will. I prayed for a wife who was in the faith, virtuous, loving, intelligent, wise and considerate, so that she may assist me in better serving the Lord. In the summer of 1994 at a meeting in Xinyang I met my wife for the first time at a coworkers meeting. She was at the meeting preparing the food for everyone. I didn't see her again until I was hospitalized in Xinyang in the winter of 1995.

As I prayed to the Lord, it became clear to me that she would be my future wife. I knew that my body was not healthy like other men and it was not easy for me to articulate my feelings, but I finally built up the courage to tell her, "Based on the standards of this world, I have no credentials. I have neither a permanent roof over my head nor land to till. My body is full of infirmities and I have no money. Furthermore, I am constantly being persecuted. I have nothing really to offer you." She was amazing. She didn't care about my inadequacies. She used her savings to help support my ministry. She even did some odd jobs to get more money to help support me.

In the spring of 1996 we were married. It was a very simple ceremony and we had nowhere to stay so we stayed in the church for two nights. On the third night I was off to work again. We were very poor and didn't have money to buy food. Over time, due to the lack of food and malnutrition my wife became very ill. We moved to Xinyang until she was better.

In 1997 she became pregnant. The timing could not have been worse. All of our brothers and sisters were being rounded up by the police, our closest partners were put in prison, and the police were looking for me and my wife.

We were also the target of the Eastern Lightning. The Eastern Lightning is a cult in Henan Province that teaches that God returned as a Chinese woman. They would capture our members and try to force them to believe in the female Christ. When our members refused they were beaten severely. Often their legs were broken, ears were cut off, and their mouths were slit. I went to visit a few of our members in the hospital. It was not even possible to report these atrocities to the local police, because the police were after us too.

On November 7, 1997, only five days after my daughter was born, I went to preach to a church in Xinyang about the evils of the Eastern Lightning cult. Outside of the house was a secret van being used by the Public Security Bureau (PSB). They had been monitoring me from across the street. We were arrested and taken to the regional headquarters where they immediately began to beat us and ask us questions. The beatings went on all night long without stopping. The next day they took us to the local prison.

The PSB found information about some of our partners and contacted them and told them that I was involved in a horrible automobile accident and was at the hospital. Everyone who arrived at the hospital to see me was captured, arrested, robbed of all their money, and interrogated.

From these interrogations the PSB was able to learn about many different secret meeting places and they immediately began their raids. More than one hundred of my coworkers were subsequently arrested.

I was placed in one of the most horrible and crude detention facilities in the country. I didn't have any warm clothes, blankets, or a bed to sleep on. The prison cell was cold in the month of November and had no heat. I had to use my hand when emptying my bowels, but there was nothing to clean up with. Many of my coworkers were in the cells close to mine. I could hear them scream out other coworkers' names when they were being interrogated. It was a horrible feeling not being able to provide comfort to them or know how they were doing. Eventually, one of my dear coworkers, Brother Wang, was transferred to my cell. I learned from him how the others were doing.

Brother Wang told me that he was stripped naked in the cold concrete cell and the fan was turned on full-speed until the cold penetrated his bones, causing unbearable suffering. After talking with him, it was evident that they were saving me for last. The PSB was interrogating everyone else to get information and they were saving me for last because I was the leader. I knew that they would be looking to give me the death sentence.

After 20 days the interrogation began. It was more brutal than I could ever have imagined. They questioned me for three days straight without taking a break. For two nights without stopping, the interrogators took turns beating me, torturing me, and asking me questions. They stripped me naked and put me outside in the cold to make me talk more. "Your group has been branded as a cult," they would shout.

I responded back, "You say we are cult, but have you any evidence of our illegal activity? Have we ever done anything to subvert national interests? What are your bases for labeling us as a cult? We are orthodox Christians. We serve God based on the Bible. You say that the Gospel Fellowship is an illegal organization, but the church is by nature an organization, one that is based on biblical models."

After more than forty days of imprisonment, they escorted more than ten of us from the Xinyang County Pingqiao Detention Prison onto a huge truck surrounded by a few Public Security vehicles with sirens blaring. The truck we were on had labels pasted on all sides with the slogan "Absolute Ban on Cults." We were paraded through the streets, and then brought to the town hall for public sentencing. All fourteen of us, including two sisters, were chained together in a row as we stood in front of the chairman's podium.

The town hall was filled to capacity, mainly consisting of university students. The chairman read out our "crimes" and announced the time span of corrective labor allocated to each one of us. Four of us were sentenced to two years. The rest were given three years. There were some in the audience that cheered when they heard our sentence. As for us, we proudly stood with our chests up and heads held high, because our consciences were clear.

From that day onward, we began a new phase of life in the corrective facility. In the beginning none of the Christians were allowed to have visitors, a rule that only applied to Christians.

The guards at the prison would question some of the inmates during meal time, "Do you believe in Jesus? If you do not believe, then you may eat. If you believe in Jesus, then don't eat. Let Jesus help you!"

This was especially tough because we were given jobs to do during the day. Failure to finish one's work would incur beatings. The work day started at five in the morning and ended at nine in the evening. This kind of punishment and work on an empty stomach made life much more difficult. When I began to look at this challenge and realized that it might go on for two or three years, I was certain that I would not survive.

In order to keep Jesus' name from shame, all of us struggled to finish our assignments. At the work site, there was no room for relaxation or casual talk. Only at night, after working hours, could we secretly gather in small groups to encourage one another with God's Word.

It was also during such sessions that the brothers would share with me the dumplings they had saved up. Since I was disabled, I could not join them at the work site, so I remained within the "Strict Scrutiny Team," where we were never allowed to have a full meal.

Not long after we had all arrived at the prison, the attitude towards us Christians had begun to change. They witnessed how we would faithfully complete our tasks, use integrity in dealing with others, and treat our enemies with courtesy. Even the supervising guards began to like us. We used every opportunity to share the gospel of Jesus Christ. I was given an early release on January 4, 1998.

I went right back to the field and began working. After my release I had seen that the church continued to experience revival and growth. It was important that we begin to train workers. We adopted three textbooks for training workers: *Lessons on the Christian Faith*, *Lessons on Christian Living*, and *Lessons on Christian Ministry*. We also used, *Questions and Answers on Christian Ethics and Morals*. Using these simple materials as well as the Bible, we conducted training sessions. We designated between twenty and thirty different training schools in different locations.

In 1999, the Chinese government rallied the nation to develop the western region of China. The church too saw the ministerial needs in the western parts of the country, which were further from the central plains and had lower standards of living. Although we had preached the gospel there and established a few churches, we found it difficult to stabilize our ministries due to distance, insufficient funds, lack of pastors, heretical disturbances, etc.

We were able to raise up thirty young couples who were willing to go and preach the gospel in western China. We were also able to identify thirty supporters who would provide the support for those missionaries.

These thirty missionaries were among the first to preach the gospel in the areas where they migrated to. They went to the minority tribes in Tibet, Qinghai, Xinjiang, Yunnan, Guizhou, Guangxi, Sichuan, Guangdong,

Hainan, Fujian, Jiangxi and Hunan.

This kicked off a vibrant era of missions and missionary training. The churches that these missionaries started also began to send out missionaries! Although our immediate focus was on the minority tribes, we also began to make plans to take the gospel into bordering nations like Burma, India, North Korea, etc.

Of all the persecution that I have experienced in China, April 16, 2002 is one of the days that I will never forget. Thirty-four co-workers and I were invited to attend a training center in Singapore called the Haggai Institute. We were told that our studies would be sponsored, but we would have to be interviewed and evaluated. We couldn't think of a feasible way of bringing the amount of leaders requested by the Institute away from the field simultaneously, for such a long time period, but eventually we agreed to meet with one of their representatives in Shanghai. I arrived in Shanghai from Zhengzhou by train on April 16. Once we arrived at the meeting location, we were told that because of security reasons we would have to immediately disperse. We were taken in groups of two to seventeen different locations. I was with one of my coworkers and soon we were placed with two coworkers whom I had never met.

The next day, April 17th, an indoctrination program began. My co-worker and I were students in a classroom of four. We were told that because of the security situation with persecution in China, instructors from the Haggai Institute had flown in and were willing to teach a class of four students. We didn't know it then, but this was an Eastern Lightning trap. The other two students were not real students, but were placed in the classroom to help the instructor and to pretend to be students.

An instructor walked into the room and began to teach. He was one of six teachers. His name was Chen. As Chen spoke I could hear the words of the Eastern Lightning teachings so I said, "What you are talking about sounds like the Eastern Lightning teachings." He explained, "The Eastern Lightning teaches from the Bible so of course there will be material that seems similar."

The instructors were so loving and friendly that I didn't suspect anything. One day in the lavatory my co-worker, Brother Shen, came up to me and told me that he did not feel good about these instructors. He felt that the females were too friendly. In our network we have strict rules about maintaining a safe distance that is socially acceptable between unmarried men and women. The females in this house were constantly coming to us when we were alone and asking for advice, comfort, and counsel.

I was asked to write a letter to all of the other co-workers telling them to listen to their teachers, do as they say, and try to learn as much as possible. I wrote the letter and it was sent out to all of the other coworkers.

However, on May 4th, after hearing an increasing amount of heresy and teaching contrary to the Bible, I stood up and openly rebutted their teaching. Everything changed. I was locked in my room and for two or three days was not given any food. Finally, they openly declared that they were representatives of the Eastern Lightning, not from the Haggai Institute. I yelled, "You guys are a group of gangsters, robbers of the church, false-Christs, antichrists, serpents draped in human skin, the filth of society! I will never forego my beliefs in Jesus Christ and follow your ridiculous teachings! I won't listen, I won't watch, I won't think, I won't debate and I won't believe!"

There was no way of getting out and I had no idea how they were going to deal with me. I knew all too well how they dealt with people who do not convert. I was prepared to be a Christian martyr.

One night, two men came and dragged me into a vehicle and told me that they were going to take me home. Instead they took me to a two-story building and locked me in a room. Guards were posted inside and outside my room. Each day the guards would preach to me, but I would not listen to them. I refused to eat or drink for fear that they would try to drug me.

They changed tactics. The male guards soon left and they sent in a female who immediately tried to seduce me. She kept grabbing me, hanging on me, and using shameless words. I refused her, yelling at the top of my lungs, "I am a Christian and a married man."

Soon she left. After some time I smashed the windows and began to yell outside. They gave up. On June 3rd, I was driven to the train station in Shanghai and dropped off. Physically I was more emaciated than I was when released from prison. One of my co-workers at another location was able to escape and reported the incident to the police. Within three days, the police were able to mobilize and hunt down the different locations of the Eastern Lightning cult and force the release of our colleagues.

We organized an open forum on June 20th. Each and every one of those who had been kidnapped shared their experiences. We mentioned how the Eastern Lightning used despicable tactics such as deception, deceit, financial enticement, sexual temptation, drugs, sexual stimulants, dreams, visions, pretense, rage, intimidation, isolation, mind control and disruption of family life. Through this forum, everyone realized that our previous understanding of the Eastern Lightning was insufficient. The attacks of the enemy still accomplished God's good purposes. God's power is revealed through human weakness. Through this series of trials, each and every one of us was severely tested with regard to our knowledge of our Lord Jesus Christ, our steadfastness with respect to biblical truth, our trust in God, and also our moral integrity. Through this fiery trial, we had matured and realized our inadequacies before the Lord.

6

THE GROWTH OF CHINA GOSPEL FELLOWSHIP

SHEN XIAOMING (continued): From the fall of 2002 until now, our church has begun to emphasize helping the poor as well as preaching the gospel. This is something that Christians must essentially pursue with fervency. However, since the church is often under persecution, Christians tend to lose heart in this regard. I thought about the church during the time of the biblical apostles. They too were being persecuted. They too underwent severe and cruel treatment. The apostle Paul encouraged the churches in Galatia by saying, "And let us not grow weary of doing good, for in due season we will reap, if we do not give up. So then, as we have opportunity, let us do good to everyone, and especially to those who are of the household of faith" (Galatians 6:9-10). The apostle Peter also once wrote to the suffering church, "For this is the will of God, that by doing good you should put to silence the ignorance of foolish people" (1 Peter 2:15).

In many churches, specific people have been designated to take charge of good works, such as repairing public roads, caring for the poor, sheltering homeless children, etc. Christians must show concern for anything that has been neglected. Christians must step up and show love to the social outcasts that no one wants to care for, even though it may not seem beneficial.

We sent out workers from our church who organized seminars that taught villagers better techniques of raising livestock, planting edible fungi, and other agricultural skills. By helping the poor we are able to glorify the name of the Lord.

I was born during the era of Mao Zedong, an

era marked by combative struggles. These struggles were targeted at landowners, wealthy farmers, anti-revolutionaries, rightists, and all Christians. Several million people were labeled as "evil" and forced to squat in cowsheds, put on tall hats, and be liable for beatings and scolding.

The era of Deng Xiaoping, on the other hand, was marked by reform and openness. Deng disliked struggles and used slogans like "No Disputes," "White Cat Black Cat," "One Country Two Systems," "Development is Solid Truth," etc. He thereby did away with many unreasonable political policies such as "Huge Pot of Rice," "Ideology of Equal Distribution," "Slice with One Knife," etc. We moved from a planned economy toward a market economy. Such reforms were a giant step forward for China. Countless people left their hometowns and migrated to the cities to do business or seek employment. There was tremendous freedom for mobility. It was amidst this change in climate that the church began to turn from looking inward to focusing outward.

The era of Jiang Zemin has been hailed as the third generation of leadership in Communist China. Jiang advocated the theory of "Three Representations," which immediately became so important that it swarmed the daily newspapers, airwaves, and TV stations. When political leaders hosted foreign emissaries, this was a mandatory topic for discussion. This "Three Representations" theory became widely credited with every sort of progress, be it the development of a small region, the prosperity of a certain market, the advancement of new scientific methodologies, the screening of a new movie, the visit of a government official, or the rescue operations of the police force. The Chinese Communist Party began to proclaim the slogan: "Keep up with the Times; Reform and Renew."

We trust that history will not go into reverse. It is only a matter of time before we see a civilized, free, and open China where the disruption and persecution of Christian meetings will be a thing of the past. The questions arise: "How will today's 'House Church' face these new circumstances? What form will she take? If the situation does indeed slacken in terms of governmental control, will she have to register? Will she register according to geographical location or as parachurch groups? What will her responsibility toward society be?" These are questions that demand serious consideration. Church and state are separate, but Christians cannot ignore politics because the two are intimately intertwined. For all these years, Christians have been hesitant in commenting too extensively on this sensitive issue of politics for fear of being swept into this complicated whirlpool. With each wave of political upheaval, Chinese Christians have tended to adopt an attitude of withdrawal. What results over time are house churches that exist passively in the world. I think that, if the government assumes an open attitude, it will recognize the legality of the house churches. Christians must be ready to reciprocate. It is not impossible to envision the house churches and the Chinese government as equal partners in dialog. We know what our stance and responsibility is: Christians are to be salt and light in the world, ready to purify the world through the Lord's love, justice and holiness. We are to be law-abiding, reprimanding sinful behavior while opposing corruption and decadence. However, we must also remember that we must not get entangled in political matters unless we are certain it is God's will. We need to maintain our allegiance to biblical principles while gradually engaging our immediate circumstances with flexibility, wisdom, and prudence.

China is a major agricultural nation. Thus, it is little surprise that the house churches of China have their roots in the farming communities. When we first started evangelizing, most people walked, while those who were better off would ride on bicycles, weaving through nearby counties and cities within a radius of two to three hundred miles. As the Good News spread and more people came to Christ, more and more local churches were established. Out of their love for the evangelists, brothers and sisters in the Lord started making financial gifts to help support them.

Before 1990, church offerings did not amount to

much. Due to the political situation, no one really taught on giving. If we even got close to a message on giving, it most likely occurred in the context of someone making a meager thanksgiving offering out of gratitude for a miraculous healing of some sort in answer to his or her prayers. Living standards tended to be poor in the villages. When even daily sustenance is a problem to be solved, the topic of giving hardly seemed relevant. After 1990, our ministries in neighboring provinces began to make progress. Since traveling expenses were naturally higher for longer journeys, stipends for evangelists also increased. This, however, put the church in a difficult position. Most of our evangelists were single and therefore without family commitments. Even those with families could not do much to support their spouse or children apart from helping out a little with farming duties. The church was never in the habit of financially supporting our evangelists due to reasons such as: (1) the poverty level of churches in farming communities; (2) the tendency to avoid slanderous labels of "profiting under the guise of religion" amidst a political environment marked by constant persecution; (3) the nature of the church as a "citizens' army" and "laity movement" whereby all ministerial positions were considered equal and professional pastors were unheard of; and (4) the lack of teaching that "those who proclaim the gospel should get their living by the gospel" (1 Corinthians 9:14).

A crisis arose with regard to church ministry and the propagation of the gospel. How will single evangelists cope once they get married? Middle-aged full-time workers in local churches face the following problems: education for their children, medical bills of relatives, repair expenses for broken-down houses, etc.

There was the case of one family who loved the Lord, received others, and opened up their home for church meetings. When brothers and sisters gathered, the husband would preach while the wife would serve the guests. As the house was on the verge of collapse, they had to borrow money to make the necessary repairs. Due to their unpaid debts, creditors often came knocking.

Failure to pay their dues would shame the Lord's name. Paying on time would mean giving up their ministries and moving elsewhere to find jobs. This couple was caught in the unenviable dilemma of leaving or staying, which eventually led to many domestic squabbles between them. Such cases are definitely not isolated examples amongst the house churches in China. It would be a tremendous shame for such unfortunate tragedies to continue where God's workers are lost to worldly pursuits.

This is an hour of critical need. When certain foreign missionaries enter China to carry out gospel ministries, they witness with their own eyes the poverty level of the Chinese house churches, and so they willingly make financial gifts to them. Some help with the daily expenses of evangelists, some express concern for needs of missionaries, while others focus on theological education.. In this manner, such foreign aid has given both invaluable support and a great impetus toward the Chinese churches. On the one hand, this generosity has become a huge blessing to churches, one which allowed for propagation of the gospel, establishment of ministry teams, migratory missions, and theological training. On the other hand, it has also resulted in parasitic dependence of church coworkers on foreign aid.

After the year 2000, the church faced crises on all sides. Funds were insufficient and many ministries already underway were unable to continue, which left the Lord's work half-finished. Numerous visions and plans were conceived but were stillborn. Due to cultural disparities, there even arose sentiments of mutual suspicion. At the present time, we see a decline in assistance from foreign missionaries. Possible reasons for this include: (1) the impression that the Chinese economy has already taken great strides forward; (2) supporters themselves encounter financial difficulties; (3) monetary aid has resulted in negative impact in certain situations; (4) givers harbor ulterior motives of furthering their own careers in China; and (5) God Himself wishes for the churches in China to mature amidst these trials.

Chinese churches must seriously consider moving

toward the goal of self-sustenance. It is a biblical teaching that churches be self-sustaining as a sign that they are spiritually healthy. Thus, church leaders should not lose sight of the fact that all members in Christ's body are mutually dependent. They can thereby better lead their members to make offerings for the sake of unity and a common vision for the Lord's ministry. Ministers would then be free of possible restrictions arising from financial dependence on outsiders; the church could avoid turmoil due to financial disputes; the government would loosen its foothold in accusing the churches on monetary grounds; and church leaders would not lose their self-esteem because of money. We trust that God will open the door to this major breakthrough.

In the beginning, evangelism amidst the farming communities began with one-on-one engagement. Those who were born-again and saved gladly shared the gospel message with those around them. God also manifested Himself through healings, exorcisms, miraculous signs, wonders, and the transformed lives of believers. The villages were unique in that governmental scrutiny was relatively loose, such that neighbors loved to interact with one another. During less intensive phases of the agricultural season, villagers would visit neighbors or relatives. In the early days in China the gospel gradually spread, to the extent that entire families were coming to the Lord simultaneously and believing parents gladly dedicated their children to the Lord's ministry. After some simple form of instruction and training, they became vibrant members of the evangelistic army. In the three months before and after the Spring Festival, villages located in the Central Plains face a harsh winter, when all agricultural activities cease. This is the lightest part of the farming season, but the busiest for Christian believers. Brothers and sisters would gather together for the commencement of "Gospel Month" events. When it first started, preachers would talk about evangelistic strategies and give out some gospel tracts.

When compared to ministry in the villages, evangelization in the cities is much more difficult. There are many differences between cities and villages: (1) time is of the essence; (2) higher cultural standards; (3) a sense of superiority; (4) reluctance to interact with others; (5) confined places of dwelling; and (6) stricter legislation on non-residents. All these factors contribute in hindering a breakthrough in our city ministries. Initially, some brothers and sisters could only minister in the suburbs. Once they had established their suburban ministries, they then hoped to make use of their relatives residing in the cities as stepping stones to minister within the city limits. Some would do business with their hometown acquaintances. Through eating, living, and working together, Christian meetings were organized. Others would begin as independent entrepreneurs. With legitimate status, not only could meetings be held at their offices, but they could also be self-sustaining. Still others would enroll as students on university campuses with the help of connections and evangelize while they studied. As entrance requirements were lowered, more high school graduates became eligible for university studies. Based on the current state of affairs, the house churches need a batch of younger brethren to further their education in universities and thereby improve the quality of church co-workers.

As for our work amongst the minority tribes, since commencing in 1994, progress has been less than ideal. Despite the obstacles of working in the minority regions of China, we have managed to establish a few churches amongst the minority tribes. We strongly believe that saving the nations is God's desire. If even western missionaries can preach the gospel to the minority tribes-people, it ought to be much easier for Chinese Christians. However, such ministry has a long learning curve where personal experiences and strategies must be constantly evaluated and revised. Various avenues of consideration are both possible and necessary for our missionaries. We continue to pray for revival in those parts of China.

In the China Gospel Fellowship, we try to focus on the unity of the Christian believers in China. Church unity is God's will. Before Jesus left His disciples, He prayed, "Holy Father, keep them in your name, which you have given me, that they may be one, even as we are one... I do not ask for these only, but also for those who will believe in me through their word, that they may all be one, just as you, Father, are in me, and I in you, that they also may be in us, so that the world may believe that you have sent me. The glory that you have given me I have given to them, that they may be one even as we are one, I in them and you in me, that they may become perfectly one, so that the world may know that you sent me and loved them even as you loved me." (John 17:11b, 20-23). The truth concerning ecclesiastic unity is familiar to every preacher and continually preached, but also very difficult to see in reality.

The house churches are not without problems in this area. Lack of communication and collective consensus on biblical truth led to the increasing independence of individual groups as each labored feverishly to spread the Good News. In the mid-1990s, some co-workers who loved the Lord took note of the disunity, and traveled all over China in a bid to gather the more influential House Church leaders for fellowship and discussion on church unity. Everyone realized the importance of unity and also agreed to maintain contact in the future. After a meeting with the most influential House Church leaders, we enacted a few important measures that would help with unity.

In recent years, we have had numerous similar gatherings for interaction but have yet to see any major results because everyone has a different understanding of unity. They consider denominations to be historical artifacts that arose under special circumstances in the past. To try to do away with denominations altogether is hardly a viable option, but neither is exalting one's own brand of Christianity while belittling brothers and sisters who do not believe exactly the same. It is both unloving and irresponsible to reject members of Christ's body who truly love the Lord. The churches in China all distinctly realize that many extremists and heretics have been shaped by a lack of fellowship and mutual correction. With regard to issues of mergers and organizational structures, we have all agreed upon three doctrinal foundations that are crucial to accomplishing true unity. Our churches are committed to being: (1) centered on Christ, (2) established in love, and (3) united in truth.

To stand firm in the truth, the church must build itself upon the foundation of the apostles and prophets, exalt the Bible as the absolute measure of truth, consult theological works of the past, and avoid private or twisted interpretations of the Word. Scripture should normally interpret itself in conformity to context. Personal insights and experiences cannot ultimately replace God's truth. We must be approved and unashamed workmen of God who correctly handle the word of truth (2 Timothy 2:15).

In twenty years of development, the House Church of China has endured much suffering. Under God's protection she has spouted roots, blossomed and borne abundant fruit. On this journey of growth filled with both successes and failures, she has had moments of brilliance as well as numerous blemishes. Facing the 21st century, we in the Chinese house churches need to reassess and transform ourselves, affirming strengths and identifying weaknesses. Armed with lessons from the past, we will hopefully be able to better plan for the future as we face even greater pressures and challenges.

The Chinese church has withstood wave upon wave of attacks. The Cultural Revolution in particular sought to eradicate all forms of religion and mercilessly persecuted Christians. Yet, not only did the church in China survive eradication, the house churches started taking baby steps on the road to maturity as she gradually gained strength. As of this day, the gospel has taken root, blossomed and borne fruit on Chinese soil. Not only have God's children not been silenced, they have grown up into the vibrant house churches of China that have gotten the world's attention.

House churches from all over China have responded to the Great Commission by fanning the fires of unprecedented missionary fervor. Today they are taking on a larger burden and shouldering a greater responsibility as they prepare to enter the harvest fields of world evangelization. This is no longer a pipe dream.

It is an actual missionary movement. God has placed the Chinese church in the midst of suffering and trial. This must somehow be part of His wonderful purpose.

The church in China must prepare for action. The harvest field ought to be the Arab world. This is a hard and tough piece of land to till. All the financial resources of the churches in western nations will not accomplish this task. Only Jesus Christ's love can transform hearts and dissolve enmity.

China has close ties with Islamic countries. For generations, they have had a tradition of forging intimate friendships with China. As China increasingly moves toward openness and Chinese churches gradually mature and unite under the banner of a common vision for global missions, the dream of past generations of missions-minded Christians in bringing the gospel back to Jerusalem may very well be fulfilled by this generation of House Church believers.

As far as I am aware, many Chinese churches are now running schools on world evangelization and studying English, Arabic, computer skills, medicine, business and Arabic culture—all in preparation to better understand and enter Arabic countries as a powerful missionary force. May we in China fight the good fight and win many souls for the Lord. Amen.

7

A BRIEF INTRODUCTION TO THE NETWORKS

Another aspect of the Chinese church that has mystified many foreigners is how churches are organized. There are several different types of churches in China which makes it hard to identify who is being talked about in any given story. Some people who have lived or worked in China (even as missionaries) will often make the mistake of thinking they are "China experts."

It is easy to see small, contained areas of China and come to the conclusion that all of China is represented in that one sample. In reality this is just not the case. Just because someone lives in Kunming for ten years and has met members of underground churches does not necessarily mean that they understand the inner workings of the super-secret House Church.

Even if someone had lived in Nanyang, a city in Henan Province that has become the incubator of today's revival in China, it would not necessarily give them the exposure necessary to become familiar with Christianity in all of China.

There are several types of churches in China because the laws that govern China and Chinese territories are not universal. To avoid confusion in this text we have narrowed down the types of churches to seven of the most common native churches found in China today, excluding fellowships like the Russian Orthodox, Korean Protestants, and other foreign registered churches.

1. The official Three-Self Patriotic Movement Church

This is the state-controlled church that has rules, clergy, and operations that are led, overseen, and implemented by the Communist Party. TSPM churches can be found in most major cities in China and are usually identified by marked buildings.

2. Official Non-TSPM Church

These are churches that are registered with the Chinese government, but do not necessarily qualify as TSPM churches. The clergy are not selected by the government, rules are more relaxed, and the government has much less oversight in these official non-TSPM churches. These churches are common in places like Wenzhou.

3. Official "Unofficial" Church

China is mostly made up of ethnic minority areas and many of these areas are setting up churches that are officially recognized by the local government, but are neither registered nor controlled by the TSPM. These churches are often found in minority areas like Yi or Miao minority villages.

4. Unregistered Independent House Church (Urban)

This specifically refers to urban areas where well-educated, well-respected members of the community meet for fellowship and unified worship of Christ. These churches are usually not connected with any other church or network and are not typically involved with outreach programs or missionary work. The majority are inwardly-focused small fellowships held in private homes where members share from the Word and worship together. These are some of the fastest growing churches in China, but still a small number of the percentage of Christians there. These churches are more common in metropolitan areas like Beijing, Shanghai, Guangzhou, or Shenzhen.

5. Underground Independent House Church (Rural/Migrant)

These unregistered churches are all over China today in the rural areas where the traditional networks do not have a huge presence. These independent churches are also strong in the migrant communities working in factories.

6. Underground Urban House Church

These are underground house churches in the urban areas which differ from the unregistered Independent house churches in that they are connected in networks and emphasize evangelism. Often they are not registered because they have either not attempted it or have tried and been rejected. These churches often have a single leader with several churches networked together, but not always. Sometimes they are an independent coalition of several churches with several leaders. These churches are very strong in places like Beijing, Shanghai, Guangzhou, and Shandong Province.

7. Underground House Church Network

The underground House Church networks are groups that have formed over time as the result of revival and intense persecution. Today these are well-organized churches that cover most of China and have a single patriarch type of leadership. Even though there are only a handful of large well-known networks, they can be found in every province and every major city throughout China.

Space does not permit us to be exhaustive enough in covering each of these different types of churches in China. Most books and articles about the Chinese church focus on Henan Province and the massive networks that have come out of that area, but the frequently overlooked networks of Anhui are as big as their Henan counterparts and are in some ways even more effective on the mission field.

It is estimated that there are more than 130 million believers in China today. More than fifty million believers are estimated to be a part of the underground house churches discussed in this book. There are more underground House Church networks that exist in China than will be covered in this book, but we will identify and explore the main well-known churches and some others that are not so famous.

In order to prevent more confusion about Chinese House Church networks, we will break them down into clear groups for easier reference. The churches will be divided into the following sections and discussed in detail:

Henan Province House Church Networks
1. Fangcheng (China for Christ Church)
2. No Name (The Five Brothers)
3. Tanghe (China Gospel Fellowship)
4. Nanyang
5. The Born Again Movement
6. Sinim Fellowship

Anhui Province House Church Networks
1. Mongfu (Blessing)
2. Zhenli (Truth)
3. Little Joe (Name concealed for safety)

Shandong Province House Church
1. Shandong Zibo Network

Other House Church Networks
1. Brother Lin (Name concealed for safety)

Wenzhou
1. Pastor Phillip

8

CHINA GOSPEL FELLOWSHIP (TANGHE) NETWORK

When introducing the House Church networks in China, it would be impractical to start with any other than China Gospel Fellowship, or simply Tanghe, because it is the most well-known underground House Church network in China. One account of the network's establishment has already been told, but now we will take a more comprehensive look at the network itself.

One of the reasons for Tanghe's fame around the world of is their huge size. Many people have estimated Tanghe to have as many as ten million believers, making it one of the largest churches in history (although Fangcheng was considered to be larger at one point).

Tanghe House Church Network contains people than most European countries, yet a search on the Internet would yield very little information about it. If one were to travel to China and ask people at the train station where to find the Tanghe Church they would more than likely get odd looks and no answers. How can a network with so many members not even be described with adequate information on Wikipedia? At the time of writing, this famed source of online knowledge only has one paragraph on Tanghe and the rest of the information posted has almost nothing to do with the network.

Tanghe Church is an underground House Church network in Henan Province that is widely accepted as being founded by Uncle Feng Jianguo before his imprisonment in 1975. It really began as a loose fellowship of believers who stayed underground and tried to survive. By the time that Uncle Feng was released from prison in 1980, a solidified movement already existed that had developed under leaders like Pastor Shen Yiping and Shen Xiaoming. Pastor Shen Xioaming has already given us a detailed account in previous chapters about the development of the underground House Church during those years.

Tanghe and Fangcheng—named after the areas they started in—have been two of the most well-known underground House Church networks in China, as well as two of the largest. These two networks, Tanghe and Fangcheng have been noted as being greatly influenced by Pastor Dennis Balcombe who is a legend in his own right.

Pastor Dennis Balcombe was born and raised in California. In 1969 he moved to Hong Kong to serve as a missionary and by 1970 he had started his Revival Christian Church in the northern area of Kowloon, not far from the Chinese border. When Deng Xiaoping began to open the doors to China, Dennis was one of the first to go and eventually made his way to Henan Province in the latter part of the 1980s. When he arrived the revival was already very much underway.

The Henan churches were greatly influenced by the charismatic teachings of Pastor Balcombe and—according to the leaders who remember those times well—these Pentecostal practices also brought challenges and division.

However, charismatic influences on Tanghe cannot be entirely credited to Balcombe. Marie Monsen is widely considered to be the matriarch of the charismatic house churches in Henan Province. She arrived in China in 1901, just when the revival meetings in Topeka Kansas were taking place. She served diligently in Henan Province and left her mark forever on the House Church in even the most remote places like Tanghe and Fangcheng.

Before Marie Monsen there was Jonathan Goforth, who was at the center of revival fires that swept through Korea and much of China in the early twentieth century. He spent some time in Henan as well and endured great hardships there, but was often accused of emotionalism.

There was also a well-known Christian general who ruled over Henan and brought peace and security to the people of Henan Province by implementing the righteousness and justice inherent in biblical teachings.

There were many other missionaries who laid the spiritual foundation for Tanghe as well and in turn had an impact on the entire House Church Movement in China.

Tanghe Network is often called China Gospel Fellowship.

As was earlier explained in the account by Pastor Shen Xiaoming, the name came from an early leader from Tanghe who commented on the teams that were being sent out to preach the gospel. He felt they were a kind of "gospel fellowship" of believers dedicated to preaching the gospel of Jesus Christ.

Of all of the House Church networks in China, the China Gospel Fellowship, or Tanghe, has been one of the most active in working with foreigners. This connection to foreign missionaries and support from foreign organizations has been one of the most prominent of all the Chinese underground House Church networks. Their fellowship has been quite inclusive in China as well. The China Gospel Fellowship is mostly charismatic, but has embraced even those who are more conservative.

Tanghe is a county under the administration of Nanyang City in Henan Province. In the early days of the House Church, there was no intention among believers there to start a church movement. Christians were just trying to survive by whatever means possible. Serving Jesus Christ and staying alive were at times mutually exclusive ideas.

The original leadership of Tanghe didn't go to Bible school and return home with grand dreams of starting megachurches that would transform their communities. They were just steadfast believers who happened to all live in Tanghe. The place where they were from became associated with the churches that were forming, growing, and spreading to other areas.

When people would ask, "Where are those Christians from?" Others would respond, "They are from Tanghe." Thus they came to be called Tanghe Church. Even though the church continued to grow in the hundreds, thousands, and eventually even hundreds of thousands of converts, they still maintained the simple name of the county where the church was birthed.

According to Pastor Chen who is one of the top representatives of Tanghe today, the beginning days of the church were full of trial and persecution. "Christians were always on the run. They would run away from the authorities and hide in the homes of their relatives. Soon their relatives would become Christians and often have to go on the run as well and go and live in the homes of their friends and relatives. The believers, both old and new, were always looking for new places to hide. That was how the gospel spread in the beginning."[15]

When China began to open in the 1980s, rumors started to emerge that the church inside had experienced growth in the face of persecution. These rumors caused many former missionaries and missionary organizations that had been praying for China to rejoice. When westerners began to peek inside China and look for any sign of believers, they soon heard about Tanghe and how the believers there were zealously preaching the gospel everywhere they went.

Foreign organizations from around the world that were hungry to gain status in China were quick to seek them out. Tanghe has probably had the most exposure to western missions organizations of any underground House Church network in China. Western missionaries and related organizations quickly came with cash in hand to help the church. They offered training, pastor support, facility funding, theological distance learning degrees, foreign mission field training and support, transportation funding, and more.

What Tanghe did not realize, was that much of the funding from western organizations came with its own price tag. When the foreign organizations offered funding, they also wanted control. Many foreign missionaries with good intentions of serving the Chinese traveled to China to train them in theology and missiology. Many of them lived with the students, ate with the students, and grew close to them.

However, when the students completed their training, the teachers or missionaries and organizations that sent them continued to communicate with them, support them financially, and even direct where they would travel, what they would do, and how they would do it. This completely bypassed the leadership of the local church. The local leadership would arrange for their students to go and get trained and gain more biblical understanding from these foreign organizations and end up losing them altogether.

The foreigner was able to provide more financial support than the local leadership and seemed to have more understanding of how to conduct long-term missions. They also seemed to be quite confident in decision making, so the students eventually became missionaries for the foreigners. It was this travesty that had led to the expulsion of foreign missionaries from China in the 1950s and 60s.

Once the foreign missionaries and mission organizations had their own spiritual militia built up in China, they began to report heavily on their activities to raise more support back in the West. Mission organizations published names, detailed pictures, locations, training goals, and progress in weekly newsletters and magazines. These magazines and newsletters were consumed by western audiences as fast as they could be printed, but back in China there were casualties.

Chinese intelligence often scanned those kinds of magazines and articles for information. Their emissaries living abroad were able to obtain many of these church and mission organization publications and glean information from them to use to locate churches, leaders, workers, and to use during their interrogation sessions.

This problem was not isolated to Tanghe, but has happened to almost every underground House Church network in China. In 2008, while Zhang Rongliang (a leader of Fangcheng Church) was still in prison, his son was in charge of the network duties. He came to meet with the writer and other coworkers in a hotel in Zhengzhou and asked us to help support a training school.

"We would like to partner with you to start a training school," he began. We were a little perplexed because we knew that Fangcheng had many training schools in China. Many of these schools were supported and staffed by very talented and dedicated foreign missionaries. "We like the way your organization [Back to Jerusalem] has always worked with us. Many foreign organizations take our missionaries and provide training for them, but then when the students graduate, they are taken away and controlled by the foreigners. We have very little contact with them and very little input about the future of those missionaries. In many ways, one more missionary to those schools is one less Chinese missionary from our church."

Many of the House Church networks have narrowed down the missionaries and mission organizations that they are comfortable working with. Newcomers are often sent through channels of middlemen that pose as decision makers. Getting to the leadership of some House Church networks is more difficult today than it was even ten or fifteen years ago.

However, Tanghe has still tried to remain as open as possible and continues to work with many foreign organizations at their own risk. A meeting with one of their top leaders, Pastor Chen, was held in June, 2011. We had to be careful with the meeting because Tanghe is one of the most monitored House Church networks in China. These days, the police may not conduct a raid, but they watch who the network is associating with and maintain a list for future use.

Pastor Chen is the current representative for Tanghe and became a believer in the winter of 1989, during a time when miracles were frequent in Tanghe. He was almost immediately enrolled into the underground Tanghe Bible School. After completing the training he was sent to minister in Hebei Province for a year, Anhui Province for two or three years, and then to Hubei for six months. He remembers clearly that this is how new believers were baptized by fire in those days. They didn't have time to get comfortable with the idea of being Christians. Once you became a believer, you were put to work right away.

Brother Yun spoke about the nature of this immersion technique used by the house churches in China during a meeting in Baton Rouge, Louisiana in May, 2011. During his sermon he stated that the longer Christians wait to be used, the less likely they are to ever be used. Brother Yun explained that in China, unlike in western cultures, new Christians are expected to immediately take what they know about Christ and share it with others. He went on to say that many people in the West feel that they must first get formal training and a diploma that supposedly gives them legitimacy to preach, and only then *might* they go out and tell others.

The immersion technique is one of the most important practices contributing to the growth of Christianity in China today. Brother Yun often points to Mary Magdalene in this instance and shows that she didn't know much about where Jesus had gone or what He had been doing since his crucifixion, but immediately went and told others that Jesus had risen and His tomb was empty.

The longer a believer waits to share his or her faith, the less likely they are to share at all, even after much study. Pastor Chen did not have to wait long before he was thrown into the heat of battle. Because workers were in such short supply, he was often called back to help carry and deliver Bibles from Guangzhou.

In 2002 he was sent to Beijing to plant churches and was able to plant more than thirty churches that are now regularly attended by more than 2,800 believers. Those churches in Beijing are now sending evangelists to Gangsu, Xinjiang, and Qinghai Provinces to share the gospel with the Muslim minorities living there.

Pastor Chen does not represent Tanghe by himself. He stands shoulder to shoulder with seven other brothers who help make decisions regarding the network. In March of 2011, all the top leadership from Tanghe came together for a strategy meeting regarding the future of the network. At that time they decided to dramatically change the way things worked in their network. Because Tanghe is so massive in size, it is difficult to adequately oversee the different aspects of future ministry. The Tanghe leadership ended up deciding to break up the representatives into eight different departments: (1) missions, (2) pastors, (3) finance, (4) children's ministry, (5) youth ministry, (6) worship, (7) education, and (8) administration.

The breaking down of Tanghe into eight different groups is new and time will tell where it leads them in the future, but it definitely shows that some of the more chaotic past is beginning to give way to order and planning. This is often the cyclic markings of revival. The beginning is usually chaotic, unplanned, explosive, and wonderful, and then the movement begins to focus more outwardly and take more deliberate steps towards future goals as it matures.

Today Tanghe has Bible schools that are connected with foreign universities to teach methodological theology. They have a training center in Beijing currently connected with a Baptist university in Malaysia that allows Tanghe students to receive legitimate university diplomas for completing studies at an underground Bible school. Tanghe was one of the first pioneers in this technique.

Tanghe cannot register with the government, not yet anyway. Many groups around the world have joined in the chant of the Chinese government to convince underground networks like Tanghe to register, but the restrictions that would be imposed on the leadership would basically bring their entire evangelical concept to a screeching halt. Understandably, they have been reluctant to do so.

This means that Tanghe cannot set up any kind of officially-recognized training facility for their students. However, partnering with foreign universities and training schools that are formally recognized and sensitive to the situation in China has allowed groups like Tanghe to provide their members with legitimate training that is formally recognized.

Tanghe today is focused on training missionaries and

sending them to countries in the 10/40 Window as part of what is collectively referred to in China as the Back to Jerusalem vision. In October, 2011, the author visited one of the Tanghe Bible schools in Beijing. The school has a business in front to act as cover. While at the Bible school a meeting was held with the instructor of the school who has been an acquaintance for several years. Christmas was approaching and we were planning on doing the "Christmas in China" project with Tanghe. The project involved hand-delivering backpacks to children throughout China that were packed with school supplies by House Church believers. Each backpack had a picture of the nativity scene and a gospel message allowing the bags to continue to minister long after they have been handed out.

While discussing the future work, the leader asked, "Do you have connections in Egypt?" Amazingly we had actually just returned from Egypt where work was being carried out with Back to Jerusalem missionaries from China. The leader went on to share that they had a missionary couple in Cairo that was working there and needed assistance. They didn't have any income and their visas had expired. The leader then provided the missionary couple's business card, complete with name, contact information, and the designation as pastor. Such openness about the ministry shows that Tanghe is definitely taking steps towards being recognized and no longer hiding in the shadows. Each year they are becoming bolder and bolder.

During another meeting in 2011, Tanghe leaders were asked what their biggest needs were. Before even batting an eyelash they unanimously responded, "Bibles."

"Bibles are one of the greatest needs that we continue to have," Pastor Chen said to in response. "Even though your organization at Back to Jerusalem has helped us with Bibles for so many years, it is still a big need. Even to get one or two Bibles is sometimes difficult when you really need to find one. We have begun to focus more on urban ministry and we know some people at the Three-Self Church who are able to help smuggle some Bibles to us, but then they often have problems afterward with accountability. When we minister to the factory workers in the bigger cities, we see large numbers of people coming to the Lord, but don't have enough Bibles to meet this need. And that does not include Bibles that we need in other languages. We have seen several Uighur Muslims come to the Lord, but they have to read the Bible in Chinese. Many of them cannot read Chinese so we don't have any Bibles to give them. We have an immediate need for one thousand Uighur Bibles."

Tanghe is focusing strongly on the Back to Jerusalem vision. They have set their sights westward to reach out to Muslim countries. They have already trained evangelists and missionaries to take the gospel to the Muslims directly to the west of China.

In 2007 there was a woman pastor from Tanghe that was living in Xinjiang Province. Xinjiang is located on the far western border of China and is mostly populated by a Muslim minority called Uighurs. Their language, customs, religion, and physical traits all indicate that they are not related to the Han Chinese, but are actually Turkic. They are an aggressive minority in China and the Uighur regions in China are always volatile. There are many other minorities in China like the Miao, Dong, Mongols, and others, but the Uighurs especially despise being under Han Chinese rule. The ethnic tension there often manifests itself in violence.

The female pastor from Tanghe was able to get a job teaching that enabled her to preach the gospel to her students. There were seven students in her class that accepted Jesus as their Lord and Savior. When the school heard about this they fired the Tanghe teacher and expelled those students. All seven students were Uighur and came from Muslim families. They were all invited to study at the Tanghe Bible school in Beijing and accepted. The Tanghe Bible teachers broke the training up into three sections covered over a period of eighteen months. The Uighur Christians studied the Chinese language, the Bible, and a vocation. After completing the training period they were sent back to Xinjiang.

For a long period of time the leaders did not hear from them. After almost two years, the leaders traveled to Xinjiang to seek out the students and see how they were doing. What they found surprised them: the students had led more than 300 Muslims to the Lord in four different cities. For those familiar with the Uighurs, this is an unprecedented breakthrough.

In 2012, Tanghe started another Bible school in Xinjiang Province. They will have twenty students in the first class. All of them are Uighurs who converted from Islam. Tanghe plans to use this school as a launching base to send graduates as missionaries into Kazakhstan, Uzbekistan, Pakistan, Kyrgyzstan, Afghanistan, and the Middle East.

Tanghe is one of the largest house churches in China. When

you see the inner workings of this church, then you can really begin to uncover the mystery of why the underground house churches are growing at such a fast rate.

9

FANGCHENG HOUSE CHURCH NETWORK

Fangcheng is a good network to examine for gaining a better understanding of the Chinese House Church. The network is considered by many to be the largest House Church network in China, with numbers being in the millions. Some estimates are close to ten million, but Pastor Zhang stopped giving out numbers years ago. Since a split among the leadership in the mid-nineties, the Fangcheng House Church has been decreasing in size and is no longer the largest network, regardless of what Wikipedia claims (as of March, 2012).

Like Tanghe, Fangcheng is also named after a county in Henan Province and is often thought of as the cradle of the underground House Church. Fangcheng was founded by one of the most well-known patriarchs of the House Church in China, Li Tianen.

Li Tianen's father was a convert brought to the Lord by the preaching of British missionary pioneer Hudson Taylor, founder of the China Inland Mission. As a devout Christian who would not deny his faith, Li Tianen was one of the primary targets of the Communist Party and his family was considered to be the product of foreign devils. Continual persecution by the government eventually led to his arrest. He was sentenced to hard labor in a prison camp because he refused to deny the name of Jesus. While in prison he took advantage of every opportunity to share the gospel with others.

After his release from prison in the 1970s, Pastor Li made his way back to Fangcheng, his hometown, to preach the gospel and raise up new leaders. There he met a young charismatic leader and Communist Party member named Zhang Rongliang. Zhang became one of Pastor Li's disciples. Li began teaching him with no idea that Zhang would grow to become one of the most well-known and respected House Church pastors in all of China.

Though Zhang Rongliang is not the founder of Fangcheng House Church Network, he is best known for leading the network and the reverse is also true—Fangcheng is well-known around the world because Zhang Rongliang is its leader.

Unlike Tanghe, Fangcheng is a lot stricter with regard to maintaining theological purity within its network. There is more control over the teachings and beliefs of those that belong to Fangcheng than those of Tanghe. This could largely be due to the personality of the leader, Zhang Rongliang. Although this may not necessarily be the case in most recent years, generally speaking this control over doctrine has been one of the characteristics that set Fangcheng apart.

Fangcheng is one example of a patriarchal House Church network where Pastor Zhang (sometimes referred to as Uncle Zhang) is the father. After his arrest in December of 2004, Zhang spent seven years in prison. His son was seen as the obvious successor in a network where the leadership style is patriarchal. However, Sister Han, a well-respected minister and preacher in her own right, was effectively the hands at the wheel.

Sister Han's face is weathered from the years of trials she has endured. She is at almost any meeting that involves the leadership, but often sits quietly off to the side and listens intently. At times she will check to make sure everyone has tea if the meeting is full of older men. She does not often speak in meetings, but when she does she is clear, to the point, and strong. Many of the younger leaders throughout China today have received training from Sister Han.

Her life has been dedicated to serving the Lord and if there is any leader not officially recognized in Fangcheng, it is Sister Han. In many ways, she was the unsung matriarch who held things together while Zhang was in prison.

In contrast to her is Zhang's son who is mostly a quiet leader who gives the first impression of being timid and soft spoken. The guiding hands of Sister Han led him down the path of leadership during the seven years of his father's incarceration and helped protect him from the unforeseen dangers that foreigners can bring.

When Zhang Rongliang was released from prison in the fall of 2011, we were very cautious to go and see him. In fact, the author initially declined an invitation to meet with him because it was our assumption that mission leaders from around the world would be banging on his door to interview him and cause a security fiasco. When it became known that a trusted friend had arranged the meeting in a secure location, the author accompanied the aforementioned Brother Ren to catch up with his old friend Zhang.

During his time in prison, Pastor Zhang had suffered from a stroke and had a terrible fight with diabetes. We were well aware of this because we had often provided financial support for his family and his medication. We also arranged for continued support of the Fangcheng church and would annually meet with his son in China to discuss needs and future goals.

We came to the interview expecting to see a fragile man with gray hair and gaunt cheeks who had been half-paralyzed by a stroke. When a healthy, younger-looking man came up to us with face beaming and firmly embraced Brother Ren we were surprised to say the least. By God's grace, prison had been good to Zhang and he seemed almost spry enough to jump right out of the room.

When we expressed our shock at his youthful appearance he moved his hand over one side of his body and said, "You see here? All of this area was paralyzed by the stroke when I was in prison. I couldn't use this part of my body at all, but the day I walked out of those prison doors it instantly healed!"

He had full use of his body and no complications from the diabetes that had given him so much trouble when he was in prison. It was phenomenal, even unbelievable had we not seen it with our own eyes.

Zhang sat down and began to talk with us. He seemed like a changed man. Before us was a humble, joyful, and introspective man very different from the firebrand we had known in the past. He sat on the far side of the couch in the small tea room and began, "You are the first foreigners to come and see me since my release from prison." This was quite shocking, considering that ambitious foreign mission workers and reporters would have been beating down his door to meet him in the past. As he sat on the couch and leaned over to Brother Ren, he looked intently in his eyes and said, "I would like to finally put a book together." From that day until the time of writing, we have been working on compiling the most comprehensive and complete, memoir of Pastor Zhang and the Fangcheng Church that has ever been written. This book should be available by the spring of 2013.

The world has understood much of what has happened

with the House Church through the struggles that were publicly played out by Fangcheng. This underground House Church network has seen many leaders taken away in handcuffs, many congregation members beaten, and even some of their dear friends executed.

In November of 2011 we had the rare opportunity to interview several of the founding members of Fangcheng House Church. Unlike leaders in many other networks, those of Fangcheng are known for being bold and unafraid of repercussions. No coaxing was required to get them to tell us about the founding of Fangcheng; they actually came ready to tell all they could remember and insisted the others sit in to correct them if they confused a date or two.

One sister recalled, between pauses to wipe away tears, the heartbreak she felt when she announced to her family that God had called her to join Zhang Rongliang's fledgling network:

> Unexpectedly, when I returned home and told my mother about the whole thing [i.e. the decision to go into the ministry], she was extremely upset. Realizing that my mom would not approve of my act upon the faith, I decided to leave home. I didn't have much of a choice. I wrote one letter to my parents, in which I expressed my strong love and devotion to Jesus; the other was to my young sister, asking her to take care of our parents.
>
> The day I left home, I felt very sad; but as Psalm 27:10 came to my mind, "My father and mother may abandon me, but the Lord will take care of me," I felt quite comforted. From that day on, I have been walking on the path of serving God.

She would go on to be used mightily by the Lord in training hundreds of Chinese missionaries for the field. Those under her care are now serving among minority tribes throughout China and even in other nations like India. The school she helped start recently celebrated its tenth anniversary. "Ten years in storms and ten years in thanksgiving," she lovingly calls that time.

Zhang Rongliang also attended that session of interviews and was more than happy to reminisce about the formative days of Fangcheng Network. What follows is his first testimony to be published since being released from prison in 2011.

ZHANG RONGLIANG: I spent seven years in jail and in 1980 I was released. After going out, I saw many thirsty souls desiring the gospel, so we started to blaze forth preaching the gospel. As we were doing so, the police heard the news and sent people to catch us and arrest us. During that time, many believers had to flee their homes because if we continued staying where we lived, we would be arrested. One escaped after another.

Later on, as we were asked how we built our team, I replied, "Oh, we have you policemen to thank for it. Because of you, our gospel team could form." When they asked when, I said, "It was when you were searching for us to arrest us." That's how we gathered together. Six hundred people were involved in our team; most of them were in debt, terribly poor, and stuck in bad circumstances. These people gathered together and became "David's Army," the army full of might to overcome nations. This is what our team was like.

Most of my companions were home-lovers, but they had to flee their homes. So when they looked back and recounted their experiences, they described themselves as "unwilling soldiers"—they were caught by God to become soldiers. Just as a Canaan Hymn puts it, "God found us from here and there." Since then, we have walked together and become a mighty gospel force in China. We wanted to go everywhere and preach.

The first one who came out in the open was Sister Ding, who was persecuted mainly by her family. The second was Brother Zheng (if you go to Henan, you will see him). He is more than seventy years old. I am the third. Then Brother Tian and Sister Han joined us too. Our team grew very quickly.

At first, there were only five old bicycles for five people; we couldn't afford anything more. Though we lacked the money, our churches were extremely consumed with Christ. I can still recall that after every meeting we had to run away because many who heard the gospel wanted to sacrifice their time and life for the cause of the gospel, but the problem was that we were unable to offer them another bicycle. Although many of them were excellent and had voiced their longing to us with tears, we couldn't help any of them and so we left with tears. We did refuse many. The number grew to one hundred as we continued to preach. This group was just like the tribe of Naphtali, who would dedicate their lives to the spreading of the gospel.

So as we see, the present China is filled with awakening souls, meanwhile it grieves us when we think about what God did in our midst in the past. It was God who brought me through it all. At that time, we sent our companions out two by two. Then we started to connect with our town, which included tens of villages, and bound them together to become one church. After the work in Nanyang had finished, we began to target our neighboring areas and helped them to build their own churches or teams.

In 1983, the government gave orders to arrest all Christians. When they got the information that Fangcheng in Henan was the center of a nationwide gospel movement, they immediately sent the police to arrest us. In that year, thirteen people were sentenced to death. As we heard about the bad news, we gathered together to cry to God for help. Deep in our hearts, we felt guilty for doing too little for the Lord.

Days later, a group of life-riskers formed. The main goal of the group was to go to extremes to save souls, even if we had to die for it. However, God kept our lives safe, none of us died. We can live so well because He is our shield.

Until 1987, we hadn't sent any workers to neighboring provinces, but afterward we went to several provinces like Hubei, Sichuan, Yunnan, and Shanxi, Hebei, Liaoning, Heilongjiang, Shandong, Jiangsu, etc.

The year 1988 was a special year for our team. There were a lot of amazing things God did in our midst. Sounds of singing, shouting and praises filled every village. It was clear that God loved the Chinese people so much. We saw many brothers and sisters anointed by the Spirit; they used the gifts they received to sow even more seeds.

Our team grew so fast that it was divided into twenty-four branches; it is a mighty army anointed by the Holy Spirit. Wherever they are, whether at the train station or bus station, whether on the train or on the bus or even while they are shopping in grocery stores or eating in a restaurant...they always share their faith. They are just like a blazing fire.

During 1998 and 1999, we started to preach to ethnic

groups in parts of China where there were still no existing churches. Our goal was to transfer Han Chinese missionaries to those ethnic groups and help them live as local residents, just as Jesus—in order to preach the kingdom of God to earthly people—came to the world and lived for thirty-three years. Many who had moved to those areas settled down and bore much fruit.

Today our church has expanded to six countries, mainly neighboring Muslim areas. We deeply feel it is the destiny to which God has called the Chinese church—to spread the gospel to all nations. In the past, many missionaries were sent to China from England; then, this commitment fell upon the shoulders of the United States, and it became the leader of the whole world.

In Deuteronomy, Moses said to the people of Israel that if they obeyed the Lord and faithfully kept all His commands, the Lord God would make them the leader among the nations. In other words, the only way to lead nations is to do what Jesus commanded—making all peoples His disciples.

For those who would like to learn more about Fangcheng and the testimony of Zhang Rongliang, a biography based on extensive interviews with Pastor Zhang and his coworkers is scheduled for publication in 2013.

10

THE FIVE BROTHERS

The Five Brothers Network is usually called the "No Name" network. This is one of the more modest groups that do not work with many foreigners and are not talked about in other forums. This network has possibly never been examined or written about before, but is one of the largest networks in Henan Province. Back to Jerusalem International has spent a great deal of time serving the believers in this network both in China and among the missionaries that it has sent abroad.

This group is just as the name suggests, there are five leaders who share responsibility for the direction of the network. In review, Fangcheng comes from Fangcheng County, Tanghe comes from Tanghe County, and Five Brothers is an underground House Church network led by five fellow believers.

The Five Brothers Network is also referred to as the No Name Network because whenever people have asked these five brothers what the name of their House Church network is called they always respond by saying, "we don't have a name." These brothers prefer not to attract any special attention and none of them really wanted to be leaders of a network in the first place. In many ways they were thrown into the role during a turbulent time for the underground House Church in China.

This House Church network came out of the Fangcheng network run by Zhang Rongliang. All five of them were some of Pastor Zhang's closest coworkers. They had been in prison together, chased by the PSB together, and endured great hardships alongside Pastor Zhang for the sake of the gospel. All five of these brothers trusted Pastor Zhang with their lives and he trusted them with his. They all saw Pastor Zhang as their leader, teacher, and pastor. He relied on them to carry out some of the most top secret missionary operations and oversee large numbers of groups. Some of them even sat on the active board of elders for Fangcheng House Church.

Needless to say, none of these brothers had initially expected to be a leader of a network. From the beginning, they had all expected to continue serving under Pastor Zhang and to see the people in China reached with the gospel of Jesus Christ through the Fangcheng Network. But things changed in the mid-1990s. In those days Pastor Zhang was notorious for his quick temper. Although in his meetings with him the author has never seen any evidence of Zhang behaving in any way other other than that of a loving, dedicated pastor, other Chinese believers that knew him well said that Pastor Zhang could quickly change moods. Perhaps those were characteristics of his younger years and his recent time in prison and health problems have calmed his temper.

In the 90s, Pastor Zhang's power and control was increasing every month in China as the church grew. The believers of Fangcheng were going out into the highways and byways to preach the gospel and new converts continued to be added to their ranks.

As before mentioned, Fangcheng strictly maintained unified beliefs and compelled others to follow. Eventually Pastor Zhang desired to establish a nationwide movement that would all fall under the leadership of Fangcheng. From this central headquarters in Fangcheng, smaller districts would be established all over China, each of which would answer directly to Fangcheng and even be expected to tithe to Fangcheng.

It is important to note that this was how all House Church networks had functioned in the early years. The main pastor or leader of the original House Church oversaw all of the growth and long-term strategic planning for the entire network. No matter how far away the sister churches were planted, it was still customary for them to answer to the mother church. Pastor Zhang was not suggesting the building of a new empire, but was merely moving to formalize ties and streamline the system, very much like large denominations in the United States.

The younger leaders in Fangcheng served on the field and saw the church growing astronomically. These younger leaders listened to the challenges that churches were facing on the lower levels and didn't feel that Pastor Zhang was listening to them. As this happened over and over it became increasingly difficult for the other leaders to ignore.

Not only were there leadership problems, but there seemed

to be a few moral failures that were taking place. Even today, most Chinese are reluctant to discuss these accusations, especially with foreigners. The Chinese prefer to handle things "in house," and to not air out their dirty laundry. As the church grew, Pastor Zhang had access to more financial resources than ever before and this newly found access brought on additional perceived problems. Whether or not there was any corruption in the way that Pastor Zhang handled the money is another matter. It was the mere fact that Pastor Zhang had sole control over these resources that led to increased suspicion being cast on him.

There were also thought to be some moral failures between him and some female coworkers, particularly with Sister "D" or Ding Hei. Sister Ding was born in Fangcheng County and became one of the first full-time workers for the Fangcheng Church. After being rejected by her family for her belief in Jesus Christ, she was adopted by Pastor Zhang's family.

The author's first meeting with Sister Ding took place in Kunming, where she is currently based. At the time she had just returned from a trip to Jordan and Israel. David Aikman's Jesus in Beijing had just come out and included her picture and information about her. When showed her picture in the acclaimed book, she just looked at it, quickly nodded in approval, and moved on to discuss the topic at hand. She has been running a training school in Kunming for several years where several westerners have been routinely rotated through as English teachers and Bible instructors. She also runs a Bible school and a vocational training center. The training center manages a small guest house that allows Bible students the opportunity to practice managerial skills in the service industry before being sent to the mission field.

Pastor Zhang and Sister Ding traveled a lot together and served in many different roles together. After a while several believers began to wonder if there was more to their relationship. Some thought it was inappropriate for Pastor Zhang to be spending so much time with a young single woman. Sister Ding eventually married and a man handpicked by Pastor Zhang (quite a common practice in the House Church), but the suspicion persisted even after she had a child with her husband.

Sister Ding insists that nothing inappropriate ever happened, but to end speculation she stopped working so closely with Pastor Zhang and set up shop in Kunming where she continues to serve to this day. She is incredibly loyal to Pastor Zhang and is a truly faithful leader. She is admired by leaders throughout China and respected by everyone who has ever worked with her. The fact that she shows so much respect and admiration for Pastor Zhang says a lot about his character as well.

Today this matter is not brought up among the leaders of the networks. If you openly ask the five brothers why they left Fangcheng Network, they will not mention anything regarding these accusations. To them, the accusations had very little to do with their split from the Fangcheng mother church. They would point to a much more pragmatic reason.

Zhang focused hard on establishing his nationwide movement where every local church established by Fangcheng would answer to the mother church in Henan and also pay a tithe. The other leaders knew that there was no practical way for them to know in Henan the detailed challenges that would arise on a daily basis in churches several thousand miles away. They also knew that there was no practical way for the Fangcheng leadership to visit these areas on a regular basis. This meant that the only real connection Fangcheng mother church would have with them would be in collecting the tithe from each church without any real association with the local problems, growth, or leadership.

The younger leadership felt that it would be better if the leadership were localized. There would be a local church established in the city that would have its own leadership and that church would be responsible for the churches that were planted in the nearby countryside.

We cannot give the real names of the five brothers because at the moment there are no other publications identifying them in the western world. We do not want to expose names and specific operations, or to hinder the progress of any of their work in any way. Their English names are Ezekiel, Barnabas, Paul, Caleb, and Joseph. Of these five, Paul is widely known as one of the most gifted preachers. When the issue of localized versus centralized leadership came up, Pastor Zhang took the firm stance that if you don't agree with him then you don't support him. In a small farm house in Fangcheng in 1995 or 1996 a meeting took place with the leadership of Fangcheng that solidified everything. Brother Ren and his long time coworker Teacher Zhao were there:

It was around this time that we saw the split take place. We were together for about two or three days discussing the challenges of the future of Fangcheng Church. There were key leaders and pastors that had traveled from far away to be at that meeting. All the key churches had their leadership represented. Altogether I think that there were about 150 leaders and pastors there at that time.

During that time the leaders came to the unified decision that localized leadership was the best way forward. It was agreed that there was just no practical way for the mother church in Fangcheng to control churches all over China in a meaningful way and expect to receive tithes. With that subject decided the leaders began to make decisions for how the future would go. They discussed how to dismantle the large-scale operation in a way that would yield more power to the local churches.

Pastor Zhang was not present at any of those meetings. I don't know why. He just didn't come, but on the last day he arrived. Everyone was happy to see him. He listened to the ideas, problems, and proposals and in one evening was able to turn everything back around.

Pastor Zhang's leadership abilities were in full swing that night. All of the top leadership was able to discuss, decide, and plan how to move forward for the future of Fangcheng. They were all in agreement. But one man, Pastor Zhang, was able to come on the last day and persuade everyone back to his way of thinking and those that disagreed were compelled to remain silent.

Pastor Zhang was closest to Paul, Joseph, and Barnabus. These three brothers comprised half of the elders of Fangcheng Church. They were three of the top six or seven leaders, so the decision they made was one of the hardest decisions in their lives. They decided to split from the mother church. For many years their identity was wrapped up in Fangcheng. They were the top leaders of the largest House Church network in China and were leaders in what could possibly be—with over ten million believers—the largest church in the world.

These three brothers made a pact with one another to daringly leave their spiritual father and continue ministry on their own; together. Ezekiel, a provincial pastor in Hubei, came along as the fourth partner. There was also a well-known local pastor in Fangcheng County who joined them. His name is Caleb and he is the oldest of the five brothers.

A sixth brother by the name of Joshua joined them as well. He is a charismatic leader and preacher who has a gift for strategy and missions work. He came alongside the five brothers and, out of true humble character, serves under Joseph. Joseph has had a life-long struggle with his health and at times is not able to carry out his duties. When this happens, Joshua rushes to his side to help him until he is well again, then returns to his own area of operation.

These five brothers set up a system of leadership similar to King Arthur's Round Table. They divided China into five different areas (six including Joshua's area) and each brother would be responsible for church growth in that sector. It was agreed that no one would make any decisions alone, but that they would all come together and decide things as a group. They work together as one team and one leadership body, although each of them is a type of network leader in their own right.

Barnabus is in charge of the work in Xinjiang and western China and rarely leaves the field. He is not always at the meetings, but has an equal say in every decision.

When Fangcheng Church split, more than one-third of its members went with the new leadership. Pastor Zhang combed through the ranks to make sure that he was not supporting anyone who was loyal to those who had left. A definite line was drawn and as a member of the church you were either on one side or the other.

From the day that these five brothers left the Fangcheng mother church, they have avoided any contact with Pastor Zhang. In many ways, Pastor Zhang blamed Brother Ren for the way things transpired. Brother Ren financially supported Fangcheng Church, but he also supported the Five Brothers. Pastor Zhang felt that the Five Brothers were encouraged to split because they knew that they had the financial support of Brother Ren to lessen the impact of the fall out, a sort of financial safety net.

Brother Ren disagrees, "I provided support to them because I agreed with their outlook on things. They were from a younger generation and they saw things a bit differently than the older generation. I listened to their hearts and their concerns and I believed that they were doing the right thing."

Brother Ren continued to provide support for Pastor

Zhang, but that financial support was suspect. It was considered to be playing both sides of the fence. However, on the day that Brother Ren and Pastor Zhang reunited after his release from prison in 2011 it was evident to everyone that Brother Ren had deep feelings of love, loyalty, and respect for Pastor Zhang. Brother Ren's support of Zhang never wavered even during his time in prison. His continued support and concern for Zhang's family, and the personal support that he provided once he was released from prison, were acts compelled by love.

The Five Brothers are aware of the feelings that Brother Ren has for Pastor Zhang and they know that Brother Ren still serves the Fangcheng mother church. Pastor Zhang has asked Brother Ren to mediate between the Five Brothers and himself on several occasions because he is the one person who holds and maintains deep relationships with everyone involved.

Recently there have been visual acts of reconciliation between the members of Fangcheng and the Five Brothers. The Five Brothers are often invited to different functions at Fangcheng church and are even asked to speak, but between the Five Brothers and Pastor Zhang there hasn't been any real lasting connection. That could change. Since Zhang was released from prison, there has been a significant change in his personality. He seems to be calmer, full of joy, and thoughtful.

The Five Brothers have gone full throttle for the gospel since they split with Fangcheng. In early 2000 they held a meeting in Burma where they set goals for the future that continue to have an impact to this day.

At the meeting in Burma the Five Brothers talked about the need for training evangelists and pastors. That led to the first-ever radio broadcast by the House Church, from the House Church, and to the House Church in China.

To create the daily radio program they used a lot of the experience they gained from running their Cassette Bible School. In the nineties the Five Brothers had a dilemma. Each one of them had helped plant churches all over their area of responsibility. So many churches had been planted that if they were to visit one church for each day of the year, it would have taken them more than three years to visit them all. They would travel around and meet with each church as much as they could, but eventually they began to record their teachings on cassette tapes. They would leave these cassettes with the teachers, evangelists, and pastors so that they could listen to them and use what they learned to teach their congregations.

This practice eventually became known as the Cassette Bible School. The recordings were actually done on DAT and were then transferred to cassette tape. Back to Jerusalem workers purchased the cassette copying machines in Hong Kong and carried them across the border to Shenzhen. Since fewer high-quality electronic items were being made in China in those days, the machines had to be smuggled in from the outside.

Eventually we put everything on CD and the International Mission Board provided us with CD burning towers. This made everything much easier. Even today after we have put everything into digital format and use simple MP3 players, we still refer to the project as the Cassette Bible School.

From the meeting in Burma also came the most dynamic children's ministry movement in the history of China, which will be covered later in this book. To this day more than a quarter of a million Sunday school teacher-trainers have been trained using the curriculum that was birthed as a result of that meeting.

The Five Brothers Network has some of the most competent English-speaking missionaries in all of China. This is mainly because of their training center set up by Brother Ren and Teacher Zhao. Ren and Zhao put a lot of resources into a training facility that would directly benefit the aspiring missionaries and prepare them for the field. The administrator chosen to run that program put together one of the most challenging and dynamic schools available for the underground House Church today.

One of the challenges for House Church missionaries is that many of them come from rural backgrounds. Many of them grew up poor in the farming communities in rural China without money to go to school. The majority of the workers in the Chinese House Church have not attended any kind of secondary education. Some have not even had the chance to finish primary school. Therefore it is almost impossible to get them formal language training or official vocational training.

The primary training center for the Five Brothers has produced some of the most capable missionaries to come out of China. Today those missionaries are serving in Syria, North Korea, Tanzania, Burma, and Vietnam and are continuing to expand to preach the gospel in other countries as well.

As the Five Brothers Network continues to grow, there are certain challenges that they face for the future. One of these brings them back full-circle with where they split from Pastor Zhang. As China grows, so does the church, and as Chinese flock to the big cities, so does the underground House Church. Today the urban centers in China are booming. Cities like Chengdu used to be sleepy little "towns" with barely five hundred thousand people, but may today boast populations in the tens of millions. There is also a mega-city in the works in Guandong Province that will combine forty-two million people into one large municipality.

The urban area churches are growing and changing the dynamic of the traditional underground house churches. The Five Brothers, though they broke from a network that they felt exerted too much control, are in fact now facing a situation where they are the ones being asked to give up control.

When evaluating the activities and practices of the Chinese House Church today, the role of Chinese culture cannot be stressed enough. The Five Brothers may have a more democratic approach when it comes to making general decisions for the future of the network, but there is nothing democratic about what goes on within their districts. They are the patriarchs and thus make the decisions. The leaders decide who can or cannot serve as leaders in their districts. They decide who will become evangelists and where the evangelists will go. They decide who will become missionaries and where those missionaries will serve. For members of the network, they decide where you sleep, how long you sleep, what you eat, and when you eat. The Chinese pastor is like the father of a family, all respect is given to him and his words are obeyed as if they were the law of the land. Unquestionable obedience is expected.

It is common knowledge that arranged marriages are common in China, but what a lot of people don't know is that arranged marriages are also the norm in the Chinese church. If you are a member of the Chinese House Church, the network leader dictates who you will marry. Not only do they select your future mate, but they will also choose where you will live together, how you will serve the church, what you will do, and how much you will make as a missionary, pastor or evangelist.

One example of this was when we were working on the North Korean border with Pastor Joshua. We had been working with five young ladies who were studying the Korean language because they were called to preach the gospel in North Korea. They studied at the school for two years and endured hardships in the process. The school was on a small farm with no heat in the classrooms and very little comfort in the sleeping area. The temperatures were almost arctic in that region, not far from the infamously frigid Siberia.

One afternoon we were together with the young ladies and sharing from the Bible with them. Joshua and his wife had spent more than two days with them giving them council and encouragement. We foreigners had walked into the meeting ready to teach the Bible but found ourselves in the tail-end of a counseling session.

Joshua pointed to one of the young ladies and said, "You are too fat. How am I supposed to find someone for you if you have gained this much weight?" I looked at the faces of the young ladies. None of them were shocked or upset. They even laughed a bit acknowledging that it was true. She did not look overweight to us. If anything, we thought the other young ladies were a bit underweight and were concerned that they were not eating enough meat to combat the cold weather.

Joshua pointed to the next girl and said, "I want you to take her jogging every morning for about forty-five minutes to lose this weight." The two girls looked at each other, acknowledged the order and nodded in agreement. The next time I saw the "overweight" young lady, she was fit and trim.

After those five girls graduated from language school and were ready for their assignment in North Korea we visited the area again with Joshua. We had a special business platform for a missionary worker at the time. We had an invitation from the North Korean government for someone who could cook. We needed a professional cook. Even though we had five students who had just graduated from language school, none of them were experienced cooks and we did not have enough time to train them.

Joshua had a member of his church who was a cook and had managed his own restaurant. He was exactly what we were looking for. We thought it would be a great opportunity to send into North Korea both a cook and a translator, but Joshua disagreed. "We cannot send a young single man onto the mission field with a young single woman," he said. He was absolutely right, but as westerners we thought the solution would be to place a third person on the team. This, however, was not Joshua's solution.

"No problem. I will just have them get married. Problem solved."

In response to the confused look on the foreign faces, he said, "No, no, I know what you're thinking. You think that they don't know each other. I tell you what. I will give them forty-five minutes to meet together before I make my final decision. How about that?"

This was so far from the western cultural understanding of love, courtship, and romance that it was hard to accept. However, the couple got married, were sent into ministry together and they are very happy together.

It is easy for westerners to look at this kind of situation and be judgmental, but we easily forget the story of how a bride was found for Isaac. We easily forget that marriages were arranged in the Bible and it is made very clear that God's will was being carried out in all those marriages. In fact, it can be argued that the Chinese methodology in this manner is more Bible-based than the western model. The western concept of love and marriage is more like a Disney cartoon and statistically has a vastly higher failure rate.

Though Joshua had a lot of control over that situation, his responsibility is much greater than that of a pastor in the western world. He travels to meet with missionaries that are about to depart for the field. He and his wife live with them, pray with them, and even cook for them. He sees that everything is provided for them and that they are lacking nothing. They only have to share their problem with him and Joshua has to carry the burden to see that all of their needs, and even some of their desires, are met.

This kind of control is typical in the House Church. Every House Church leader plays the part of a patriarch. Some are more involved than others, but they all have this practice. At training sessions with Chinese House Church missionaries it is standard procedure for us to tell them why they are at the training and what they will be doing. We don't do this as an introductory formality, but because often nothing was ever communicated to them.

Has your pastor ever called you and said that he had a plane ticket for you to fly to Hong Kong and told you to be at the airport the next morning for the flight then immediately hung up without conveying any other information? This is common in the house churches in China. It is an everyday practice for a worker in the underground church to get a call with directions to be somewhere at a certain time with no explanation. Although this is great for security, it does very little for an information-driven individual.

In the winter of 2011, we had a team from China that was going to study for six months in the Philippines. When the team of ten students arrived at the airport in Hong Kong none of them knew what they were there for. They were merely told to board a flight to Hong Kong and then someone would be there to meet them with further instructions. The ten Chinese, most of whom had never met each other, boarded their flight to Hong Kong without question.

When asked how much they knew about what lay ahead of them upon arrival, none of them knew they would be going to the Philippines, nor did they know they would be gone from China for six months. They also had no idea they would be doing missionary training with foreigners. One of them suspected she would be going to Vietnam to live. Even at that she had only packed a single handbag. They didn't even know what climate to be prepared for.

Whether or not we agree with this method does not matter. This type of seemingly-blind obedience is one of the contributing factors to why the church in China is growing at such a drastic rate. Their churches have a patriarchal system that fits their culture, works for them, and is having an impact on the entire world in ways that are difficult for the western-trained mind to grasp.

The urban areas, however, are more independent, so the Five Brothers are facing this reality when working and overseeing the churches in those regions. The educated, independent minds of today's urban Chinese are generations away from the traditional rural areas of China. How the Five Brothers Network adapts to these new challenges will undoubtedly determine their future.

11

THE CAVE

One story that has never been told before is about one of the most effective training centers in all of China during the early 1990s. As the House Church in China grew, so too did the need for competent leaders. However, many of the Chinese didn't even have Bibles, let alone Bible training.

One major reason for the lack of Bible training was simply that there weren't enough qualified Bible teachers. So many Chinese served God according to what they heard older people in the villages say who claimed to be believers. They also had different perceptions of God that they had deduced from dreams.

Even if there had been enough teachers, there was still a shortage of places they could safely teach at. Finding a place to train missionaries in those days was much more difficult than it is today. If Christians met together in secret, not only did they have to watch out for the police, they had to ensure that even the neighbors didn't see or hear anything. A zealous Communist neighbor could report any activity that seemed suspicious. Congregating in unauthorized meetings was strictly forbidden in China in the early days probably because it was under similar conditions that Mao Zedong planned his overthrow of the government. He wasn't going to risk the same thing happening to him that he had pulled on others.

While working with many leaders all over China there was one memory that a great deal of them shared: "the cave." Even groups from the Anhui networks had traveled to Henan Province to train in the cave.

An underground cave that had been dug out by hand was where thousands of the Chinese Christians had been prepared for the mission field. Far from looking like some glorious missionary training center, it was crude, cold, and utterly uncomfortable, but it was the place where so many Chinese chose to be trained.

Sister H's key role in transforming the underground House Church movement has never really been mentioned before. She was the one with the initial vision for the cave that eventually made a huge impact on the history of the entire Chinese House Church. Although she was totally unaware of it at the time, God was going to use her in ways she could have never imagined.

In the late 1980s Brother Yun had very few people that he could rely on to hide him and his family from the authorities. The persecution from the government was intense and it was taxing on his whole family. Sister H prayed for Brother Yun on a regular basis while he was in prison and was deeply concerned for him and his family. Many nights she was unable to sleep because she was up praying for him and asking God to keep him safe.

Brother Yun's preaching was full of joy and without compromise, but his family had been paying a huge price for the work. His wife and children were constantly being harassed and publicly humiliated for his "crime" of proselytizing in China. Even when he was not in prison, he was rarely home. Deling had to keep the household together all by herself.

In 1989 the revival began to spread uncontrollably to other areas as well. The gospel was moving from the rural farming communities to the more affluent cities where university students and even government officials were getting saved. In Brother Yun's village alone there were several Communist Party members who had come to the Lord and began to preach. As the multitude grew, so did the demand for shepherds to lead them. Pastors and preachers like Brother Yun were so busy that they did not have time to eat or sleep, let alone see to the physical and spiritual needs of their families.

The people were so hungry for the gospel that they would pack into small spaces to hear the preachers and wouldn't leave. The pastors would have to be passed over the crowd in order to get to the next meeting. The leaders realized that they could not carry out this task alone and Deling appealed to her husband to take time to rest, pray, and be with his family.

Brother Yun and the leaders began to pray for guidance and vision. Little did they know that God had already heard their prayers and was preparing a place for them. The answer would not come from a westerner or a successful businessman, but from a humble prayer warrior.

Sister H owned several homes that were built in a traditional Chinese style. Anyone who has ever visited a traditional Chinese home will recognize the unique layout. Today most Chinese live in high-rise apartments, but prior to the urbanization of China there was a longstanding tradition in the way houses were built and used.

Every Chinese home had a courtyard that was surrounded by walls. A quick visit to the Forbidden City in Beijing will give one an idea of this concept, but on a much larger scale of course. Chinese traditional homes always have a wall giving privacy to the courtyard. There are usually three different living quarters that are in the shape of a horseshoe with the most senior family members living in the center home and the younger families living in the homes on each side.

Sister H, who was born and raised in Nanyang, had one of these traditional Chinese homes in a place called Jingwa Town in Nanyang County. Her house was at the base of a mountainside. She was the first person to become a Christian in her family and that took place in 1979 when she was about thirty years old. Her mother knew that she was an angry young lady who was always getting into fights. When Sister H's mother saw how she had changed into a loving servant of God, she too immediately came to the Lord.

"My mother knew that it must have been a miracle. Anything that made me turn from a hateful angry person into a loving person had to be the work of God and my mother immediately became a believer."[16]

God began to tell her to use her home as a place of refuge for Brother Yun. Beside her stove in the kitchen was a stack of firewood that she would use for cooking and heating the home. She had the idea of removing the firewood and creating a small secret space in her home big enough for one person to enter. The entrance could then be concealed with firewood.

As of February, 2012, Sister H is a mother of five and grandmother of eight. "I remember a need during those early years to create a secret hiding place for books and things like that. So my husband and I dug out a small place in the side of the mountain and covered it with rocks so that it would look like the rest of the wall."

Behind the area where the firewood was kept was a soft limestone area in the mountain that allowed for Sister H to dig out this small space by hand. She dug out an area that was big enough for two people to squeeze into.

God moved on the hearts of Deling and Brother Yun to take a time of rest and just pray before the Lord. Sister H's small cave seemed to be the safest place for that. Brother Yun traveled back to Henan, met with Sister H, and began to use the prayer closet she had prepared.

The prayer closet did not remain a prayer closet for long. Brother Yun loved the idea of having a place to go and pray, but anyone who is familiar with him knows that he loves to be around others. He always shares everything he has with others. Soon he began envisioning this prayer place being used for much more.

Brother Yun began to express the need for training of others and he also emphasized the fact that the leaders needed to be more attentive to their own families. He argued from Scripture that one who does not properly care for his own family cannot possibly take care of the church of God (1 Timothy 3:5). In the life of a Christian, God must always come first, family second, and ministry third. Unfortunately several House Church leaders opposed Yun in this teaching and the problem of ministers choosing ministry over family continues to be one of the major weaknesses of the Chinese house churches to this day.

Soon the work to build the prayer place into a larger area for people to pray and train together was beginning.

Brother Ren remembers well when the cave was being constructed, "I sat down with the Chinese brothers and sisters and we designed the training facility in the cave. My background was in construction engineering. I focused on the need for electricity, air circulation, and structural integrity. We designed the cave with the idea that we could fit more than one hundred people inside. I remember that we would sleep in the house and crawl through the secret door by the oven during the time that we were building it. We began to call the mountain *Tian Shan* (Heavenly Mountain). Everybody would put dirt in their pockets or rocks in a bag or backpack and take a walk towards the other village and empty their bags and pockets along the road away from the construction site."

There was a nearby rock quarry that masked a lot of the activities, but no one wanted to take any chances. Even though the debris from the cave construction would have been largely unnoticed because of the excavation taking place at the quarry, there was no room for error. This place would need to remain a deeply-guarded secret. To prevent infiltration, only the top leadership and those closest to them could be a part of this training facility.

Small tractors were also used to move the rocks, but that could only be done at night. All the digging was done with crude hand tools. There were only four people who were responsible for building the entire cave—Sister H, her husband, her husband's friend, and her son. Sister H and these three men hammered away until their hands were cracked and bleeding. Their joints would still have the vibrating sensation of pounding a hammer into rocks even hours after they had stopped. They were unable to enjoy a good night's sleep during those days, but the hunger for having a place people could come to and pray, sing to the Lord, and learn more about Him drove them to work around the clock.

They would use a metal chisel and bang away until they had chunks of rock large enough to shovel out. If they hit an area of soft rock, they would stop hammering and change direction. They used the areas that felt safe and stable. Many believers encouraged them to enlarge the area even more after they had finished.

"It would not have been safe to make it any larger," Sister H said. "The cave felt pretty safe and secure, but if we would have gotten greedy and tried to make it even bigger, then we could have had the entire thing come down on us."

"We would send as many people as possible with rocks and dust from the cave," Brother Ren recalled.

Even today, Sister H's hands are rough and callused from hard work.

"If the police would have known what we were doing," she said in a recent interview, "They would have... (she put her fingers up to her head to signal a gun being pointed at her temple)."

"They would have killed you?" asked the interviewer.

"Absolutely. During those days if the police would have known that I had a secret cave where I hosted meetings like this they would have executed me."

Joshua, one of the House Church uncles mentioned in this book, also visited the cave many times. "In the beginning of the 90s we would have our training there in the cave. It was in this cave that many people fell in love with the Lord. We had many precious times of prayer. Many of the missionaries who were trained in this cave went out and served the Lord full time. We were so excited to finally have a safe place that would allow us to learn, sing, and worship without fear. We would even abstain from eating food and drinking water so that we did not have to leave the cave to use the bathroom. There wasn't any place inside the cave to go to the bathroom. When you went in, there was no way to leave until everyone left, so it was important that you planned around those times."[17]

When the cave was completed it was able to fit more than one hundred people. The door was about one square meter located in the bottom of the wall next to the floor behind the wood pile. To get to the secret cave one had to go into the kitchen and move the wood pile out of the way. There was a blanket that was often used to hang over the hole and looked like it protected the wall from the wood pile.

To get into the cave one would have to crouch down and fit through the one-square-meter hole. Through the hole one would crawl or scoot about ten meters down a small corridor that led into the main room. The ceiling was about two meters high in the highest spot. The measurements were not exact because there was not one single right angle in the entire cave. There was increasingly less head space closer to the outside edge.

There was always the challenge of keeping noise from coming out of the cave. A thick blanket thrown over the hole was used to keep the sound from getting out, but that also restricted the air flow.

"Most of the time we would only train for three to four hours at a time inside the cave because of lack of fresh air," Joshua remembers from his time there.

In the beginning they used candles to provide light, but this was not a long term solution. Brother Ren used his engineering skills to solve the problem. He arranged for a generator that would provide for the lights and a fan.

"We could not use the local grid for electricity. The local officials would notice right away that an unusual amount of electricity was being used by a small family. This suspicious activity would have led to the discovery of the cave, so we needed a way to provide the electricity. I arranged for a gas-powered generator to be used instead."

A fan was used to circulate the air that did very little to combat the dust and dirt in the air. Brother Ren also arranged for a dehumidifier. When the cave was new the students and teachers would come out of the cave after a day of intense training and look like zebras, their faces black and white as if they had been working in a coal mine all day. A large pipe was later installed that would allow more air circulation.

Soon after it was built and began to be used as a training facility, foreign preachers and missionaries began to come and teach in the cave. This presented an additional challenge for security, but the leadership was hungry for the Word of God. Around the mid-nineties cell phones began to be used. Not many Chinese had access to cell phones in the early days and any foreigner with a mobile phone was closely monitored. A rule was quickly made that no mobile phones were allowed in the cave. Foreigners were told to remove the batteries from their phones so that they would not give off any signals to the PSB.

Not long after a visit from Pastor Dennis Balcombe, the PSB was able to obtain video footage of the underground cave from the inside. The police did everything they could to locate this cave. Several leaders were arrested and interrogated to obtain information about its whereabouts, but the location was never discovered.

"There were some close calls," Brother Ren remembers. "Several years after we completed the cave, a Finnish organization donated a solar panel that we could use for electricity. This of course was much quieter than the gas powered generator. One day a patrol officer was walking through the neighborhood when he noticed the solar panel on Sister H's roof. During those days not many people in Nanyang had solar panels on their roofs. He came around to Sister H's main entrance and confiscated it. He never followed the wires from the solar panel to see where they led. If he would have followed those wires it would have led him right to the cave!"

The cave was used for about ten years. "I would estimate that there could have been as many as twelve thousand missionaries trained in there," Brother Ren said. "It was one of the safest places that we had during those days for training. You could sing, you could dance, and you could preach without much fear of being heard or caught."

"We had a lot of amazing times in that cave," Joshua said as he reflected over his cup of tea at an interview. "You know, I saw my first black person in that cave. I don't remember who arranged for him to speak and teach. I don't know if he was a black American or an African. All I remember was that I had never seen a black man before. I found it amazing that so many people from all walks of life came and shared the Bible with us in that little cave. Brother Ren and Teacher Zhao came to speak there many times and I have fond memories of those days. That is where I learned so much about the Bible and much of what I learned in those days I teach here in my school today."

The police never found the cave. Sister H recalled, "The police were looking and looking for the cave, but they never did find it. Zhang Rongliang had visited the cave with some of his partners. Soon after he left, word began to circulate that the police were intent on tracking him down and arresting him. My husband and I felt that the cave had served its purpose. We felt that ten years without being discovered for a place so big was a real miracle. We also felt that there could be a chance that Zhang Rongliang would be caught, tortured, and forced to tell about our cave. With so much on the line, we decided that it was time to destroy it. Around the entrance to the cave there were wooden supports. We pulled out the wooden supports and let the entire entrance collapse, closing off the entire cave."

In those days there were about three hundred people living in that area. In 2000, the rock quarry workers came in and excavated the mountain. Today there is nothing there. The land is flat and barren. There are no new houses or any building projects where the mountain once stood, but the memories of the cave that was there during the 90s still echo throughout China.

Fig. 1 Taken at the historic meeting in Burma where representatives from almost all the major Henan networks were present (2000)

Fig. 2 Chinese House Church evangelists training in a cave

Fig. 3 Bibles being delivered in the 1990s

Fig. 4 A Bible delivery van in the 1990s

Fig. 5 Zhang Rongliang with a coworker in Henan

Fig. 6 (Left to right) Enoch Wang, Zhang Rongliang, and Brother Yun

Fig. 7 Brother Yun with family in Nanyang (1993)

Fig. 8 Brother Ren with Peter Xu and his sister

Fig. 9 A class at one of Mongfu Network's missionary training centers

Fig. 10 Inside a Mongfu Network Bible school

Fig. 11 A Mongfu Network missionary in training

Fig. 12 A Mongfu Network leader shares a meal with trainees

Fig. 13 Mongfu Network evangelists preaching the gospel in the minority areas of western China

Fig. 14 A Mongfu Network evangelist delivers Bibles

Fig. 15 A Mongfu House Church worship service

Figs. 16, 17 Henan House Church leaders in training worship in
Sister Han's secret cave

Fig. 18 Brother Yun in the Henan cave

Fig. 19 The site where the Henan cave used to be

Fig. 20 "Little Joe"

Fig. 21 Pastor Philip of Wenzhou Province

Fig. 22 Xiao Min, writer of the Canaan Hymns

Fig. 23 A worship service in Wenzhou

Fig. 24 Sister Huang strategizing with Chinese Sunday school teachers for the Dove project

Fig. 25 Sister Huang introducing the Dove curriculum to Anhui House Church leaders

Fig. 26 Children praying during a Dove training session

12

THE BORN AGAIN MOVEMENT

The "Peter Xu" Network is the name we have chosen to use for this underground House Church, although the network has also used many other names in the past. The church has also been known as the Born Again Movement, the Weepers, the Criers, the Full Scope Church, Word of Life, and New Birth Church.

The Born Again Movement was founded by Xu Yongze, known as Peter Xu in the West. The author has known and spent a considerable amount of time with Peter Xu and his sister Deborah. Whenever Brother Yun is in California for speaking engagements Peter Xu and his colleagues always end up staying in his hotel room, often arriving at the hotel at all hours of the night with guests wanting to pray with Yun. Peter Xu has been called the Billy Graham of China and in many ways his testimony is just as compelling as that of the "Heavenly Man," Brother Yun.

In 2001 he was able to flee China and find political asylum in the United States. Shortly after arriving in America he settled down in Buffalo, New York. He had been through a lot by that point in his life. Peter's first wife dissolved their marriage because she could not stand the long periods of separation she had to endure. Those periods were not like those of most women married to itinerate evangelists or military personnel. While most wives may experience separation for a few months or even a few years, Peter Xu's wife went without seeing her husband for 23 years.

Peter waited to be reunited with his wife, but their marriage seemed irreparably over when she remarried. Xu was then remarried in 1996 to a bride much younger than him, a move that presented a lot of challenges for Peter Xu's coworkers in China. When he moved to Buffalo, New York, his family was in dire straits. Brother Ren remembers going to visit him during the first year he was in America.

"Peter and his new wife had just had a baby," recalled Ren. "They did not have enough money to buy new diapers so they attempted to hand wash the disposable diapers in the sink and hung them out to dry—which proved to be an impossible task." Brother Ren gave them some financial support to help with their expenses in the US.

Brother Ren is one of the big differences between Peter Xu and Brother Yun. Xu did not have a foreign counterpart to help him adjust to life outside China like Brother Yun did. Brother Ren took on the role of Brother Yun's pastor and advisor and helped him cope with living in the West.

Brother Ren ensured that Brother Yun was able to receive a monthly salary to provide for his family. Yun's speaking engagements were arranged by a responsible mission board, taxes and registration of every activity were done according to law, and ministry partners understood the mission and vision of the Chinese church.

Peter Xu did not have that support in the US. He was swimming in shark-infested waters without a raft to cling to. The only reference that Peter Xu had prior to coming to the US was an illegal, unregistered, underground, covert church in China. The idea of having a registered non-profit organization for supporting Chinese missions was a totally foreign concept.

Xu had no way of really discerning between the churches and organizations that wanted to truly partner with the Chinese church and those that merely wanted to raise funds for their own projects. Many groups in America saw Peter Xu during the time he was financially vulnerable as someone they could take advantage of to raise funds for their own domestic visions and projects. Once Peter Xu had served his purpose in their eyes, he was thanked, patted on the back, and sent out the door.

Eventually Xu moved to Los Angeles where he continued to raise awareness about the vision of the Chinese House Church. He had problems with the idea of registration in the US and maintained many of the habits he had developed in China. According to Joy In who worked together with Peter Xu for several years in Southern California, "Peter never really understood the idea of registering with the government in America. At the end of the year I was getting all of these requests from donors who needed donation receipts from us for their tax returns and we had nothing to really give them in return. Peter Xu thought that is was just a matter of sending a thank you letter to those who had donated."

Today Peter Xu lives in Colorado where he has started a new mission with new staff called Back to Jerusalem Gospel Mission. It has been a hard road for Xu, full of ups and downs. He has taken a few falls along the way and continues to believe in the Lord for his strength and provision.

Like Zhang Rongliang, he was also a disciple of Li Tianen. Peter Xu, however, immediately saw a need to train and send out disciples to reach the lost in China. Peter Xu is unique in this way. While the other networks started without an initial intention to go beyond their own homes, Peter Xu was very deliberate in focusing on outreach beyond the borders of Henan. He was able to immediately sense the Spirit pushing him toward the outer reaches of China.

The other networks were named after the counties that they came from. Fangcheng, Lixin, Nanyang, and Tanghe networks were all named after the counties they started in. These massive House Church networks were not deliberate from the beginning, but Peter Xu's House Church network was different. It was a deliberate movement.

Whenever you spend time with him or read his story it becomes clear that there is something deep in his spirit that drives him. Today, even in his later years, he comes across as calm and friendly, but there is a spark in his personality that is almost combustible.

His life has been packed with adventure and drama. Paul Hattaway, the coauthor of *The Heavenly Man*, sat down with Peter Xu and attempted to write a biography about his life. The book has never been published, but if it ever is, it is bound to be one of the most riveting stories ever told.

Now in his seventies, Xu has no intention of slowing down. There will be no retirement for this man of God. His new organization in the US is working to build partnership and participation between the churches in the West and East.

Peter Xu is a fourth generation Christian. He was a rebel from the beginning. When fanatical students were swarming campuses with Communist propaganda and refused to tolerate any dissent, Peter also infiltrated the same campuses with the gospel of Jesus Christ. During that time, the violence of the student movement in China was intense. It can best be seen through the story of Yao Ming's mother. Yao Ming is a world-famous Chinese basketball player in the NBA. His mother was part of the revolutionary guards—a kind of shock troop movement that would carry out the most extreme acts of persecution and cruelty on a horrific scale.

Yao Ming's mother was one of the most vocal leaders of that movement and the one whom many feared the most. She led the charge against her former basketball coaches. In one of her more mild actions to discipline a supposed female dissident, she cut off the woman's hair. She led angry mobs onto campuses like those that Peter Xu was ministering on.

Preaching on a vocational campus in China was a huge risk, not just for Peter Xu, but for anyone who participated. Peter Xu started the group as a reading club and used the club as a way to introduce students to the Bible. When the Communist regime decided to conduct a sweeping raid on Christians, Peter Xu was one of the top people on their radar. He was soon arrested in 1963 and questioned for forty days straight. He was eventually sent to prison four more times.

Peter Xu's strong leadership is one of the many factors that contributed to an autonomous underground House Church. As the doors to the West began to open, Christian organizations began to slip through the cracks to see how the church in China had developed. They soon felt compelled to become more than observers and many had a desire to help their brothers and sisters in Christ. In the 1980s Christian books other than the Bible began to appear in China. Each denomination had their own idea of what the church in China needed.

> These booklets told us we must worship in a certain way, or that we must speak in tongues to be a true believer, or that only if we were baptized in Jesus' name (instead of the name of the Father, Son, and Holy Spirit) could we be saved. Other teachings focused on extreme faith, still others argued for or against the role of women in the church.
>
> We read all these booklets and soon we were confused! The churches started to split into groups that believed one thing against groups that believed another. Instead of only speaking for Jesus, we also started speaking

against other believers who didn't conform to our views.[18]

The church in China was being bombarded with the teachings of various foreign denominations. This was difficult for them and raised a lot of questions. Many of their colleagues had died in prison for the name of Jesus, yet had never been baptized in the name of Jesus. Did they go through all of that suffering for Christ only to be lost through a technicality?

There were many founders of the church who had been persecuted and martyred in the 1960s and 1970s, but had never spoken in tongues. Were they to perish in hell for never having spoken in tongues?

And today, anyone familiar with the House Church movement cannot deny the overwhelming number of female pastors, teachers, evangelists, and missionaries. How were they to fit in with the foreign doctrines in these booklets?

Peter Xu was one of the first to stand up amidst this mass confusion and seek unity with his fellow believers in China. It was through his leadership that a movement of unity among the Chinese underground house churches was formed.

Brother Yun tells the story of how the leaders of two major movements in the Chinese House Church came to meet together in his book *The Heavenly Man*.

When they had arranged for a secret meeting, they had all traveled far and taken many security measures to be together. This was a meeting that the Public Security Bureau would have loved to know about. It would have saved them a lot of trouble to be able to find the leaders of such major underground movements all together in one single meeting.

After they had gathered together, Peter Xu received a word from the Lord that he was to go and wash the feet of Zhang Rongliang. "Zhang was praying with his eyes closed when Xu knelt down in front of him and started gently to take his shoes and socks off. Zhang opened his eyes and was amazed. He couldn't believe the great Xu Yongze, leader of the largest House Church movement in China, would ever kneel down and wash his feet! Zhang cried out and wrapped his arms around Brother Xu in a warm embrace."[19]

This one act performed by Peter Xu unified two of the largest underground House Church networks. The Born Again Movement was joining hands with Fangcheng and the two of them would act as a beacon for unity for the other House Church networks to witness. This moment of unity cannot be overrated. The two leaders, Xu and Zhang, had very strong personalities and leadership characteristics that are so similar that they were bound to butt heads.

The Born Again Movement and Fangcheng came together and called themselves the Sinim Fellowship. Sinim is often thought of as the biblical name in prophecy given to China. The name Sinim comes from Isaiah's prophecy in Isaiah 49:12, "Behold, these shall come from far: and, lo, these from the north and from the west; and these from the land of Sinim (KJV)."

According to Brother Yun, this collaboration led to the forming of a fellowship that included most of the underground House Church Christians in China. "In October 1996, five men were elected to be the first elders of the Sinim Fellowship. They were Brother Xu Yongze (Peter Xu), who was voted the Chairman, Zhang Rongliang, Wang Xicai (Enoch Wang), Shen Yiping and myself (Brother Yun). Each man represented a different network."

This fellowship embodied the unity of several million believers throughout China and caught the attention of the world. These fellowships in China were unified. Each network was able to maintain their own set of beliefs according to their interpretations of the Bible.

Not many churches in the world are strong enough to obtain true unity with other believers in Christ without compromising the integrity of their beliefs. Unity can exist in desire, but it does not exist in fear. The underground churches desired to be unified together in Christ, but why not with the official church? All of these brothers were a part of the underground House Church, but also had the opportunity to unite with the official church (TSPM) as well. Why didn't they do so? If they truly wanted unity among the believers in China why wouldn't they chose to be unified?

The leaders of the TSPM in China say things like, "Jesus is alive because He lives in my heart." Westerners hear this and they are overjoyed and ready to see the Chinese church unified. If the official church in China believes in Jesus and the underground church believes in Jesus then that is all that matters, right?

Many of the words spoken by TSPM leadership have a double meaning. The idea of Jesus living in the hearts of the believers in the way that the TSPM uses the phrase is much like the belief that a good person who dies lives in the hearts of those who carry on with the vision of that deceased person.

For instance, if you lose a father who had established a foundation you might make a speech at the funeral like, "Today the world loses a good man who has done many great things through this foundation. We will carry on the work that he began and in this way he will remain alive in our hearts." This is not all that it means to a true Christian who believes that Christ resides in our hearts, but it is what is meant by such statements by the TSPM. The Christians in the Born Again Movement had a leader who wanted to be unified with fellow believers in all of China as well as those around the world, but he could not trade unity for integrity and allow his flock to be fooled into believing a fake gospel.

Even today, many of the house churches have continued to follow Peter Xu's lead on this matter. Many western leaders around the world have tried to mediate between the government and the House Church of China to get them to register. Luis Palau is a well-known mission strategist and evangelist credited with introducing to the mission community the term "10/40 Window."

In 2005, Palau spent some time visiting Christians in China. During the visit he attended a worship service in Beijing with former President George Bush and made some strong statements towards the House Church Christians.

> "Mr. Palau told reporters that some reports of religious persecution are unjustified," The Times reported, drawing from a transcript it obtained via the Web. The newspaper stated that Palau "suggested that China's unofficial churches should register to 'receive greater freedom and blessings from the government.'"
>
> The Times reported that Palau "then compared church registration in China to American tax law. 'Even in the United States, you can't get away with defying order,' [Palau] said. 'I feel that registering is a positive thing for the followers of Jesus. Believers should live in the open, especially when the Chinese government offers it.'"
>
> Palau continued, "Jesus said that we are the light of the world and that we should not be kept hidden or in the dark. Therefore, believers should share their faith openly. If I were Chinese, I would definitely register. Not registering

only lends to misinterpretations and misunderstandings."[20]

Mr. Palau later retracted the statement, but even today on his website—almost seven years later—he still believes that the underground House Church in China should register. After a trip to China in 2010, his official website says, "Palau encouraged Mr. Wang to make it easier for churches to register in China, suggesting that many do want to register but don't meet the current government registration requirements. Mr. Wang introduced the idea that registration brings churches under financial accountability and oversight, much like those in America. Palau agreed that financial transparency is important for all groups serving the public."[21]

Luis Palau is not alone. In May of 2008 one of the top directors from a well-known international ministry asked to meet with the author at Hong Kong's airport to discuss something.

"I just wanted to discuss something before you hear about it on the news," he said. His boss, Franklin Graham, had just preached at several churches in China and was present when the earthquake hit Sichuan. We had been working together on delivering shoeboxes full of gifts for children in China for about six years and had a great relationship.

While Franklin was in Beijing he had met with government officials. In response to a question about evangelism during the Beijing Olympics, he said that he would not agree with any foreign missionary or mission group that chose to break the law by sharing the gospel in China. "I would be against any groups that would be coming in and encouraging people to break Chinese law," he said.[22]

It was quite ironic for him to say that after having worked together with our team of Chinese lawbreakers for so long. He of course was just saying what needed to be said in front of the Chinese government officials who had gone out of their way to arrange his tour.

That year ended up being our last year of working together. After the Sichuan Earthquake, Franklin sent an official letter to the Chinese Embassy introducing the idea of delivering the shoeboxes to children in Sichuan Province. Before this there was no official connection with the program and Franklin Graham's organization. Once he solidified his plans to work through official channels, Back to Jerusalem International was forced to pull out and support his ministry from a distance. "We think what you guys are doing in

China is great, we just can't join you in it. You work with the officials and work your way down. We work with the grassroots church and work our way up. One day we will meet in the middle."

When asked if Franklin was asked by the government to say or not say anything while preaching in China, the director's response was, "No, not really. There was one thing. They said that he should not mention the underground House Church. They acknowledged that it existed but requested that it not be mentioned."

Franklin's words of course were greatly criticized by other mission organizations working in China together with the underground churches. Franklin also posted the laws of China on his website as he had promised the government officials. In their listing of laws, State Religious Affairs Bureau Order No. 5 was curiously missing. This order from the State Administration for Religious Affairs states that a Reincarnation Application must be filed by all Buddhist temples in order to be recognized when they return. If a Buddhist monk reincarnates without his permit he can be charged with a crime.[23]

Westerners who are not that familiar with China are not the only ones putting pressure on the Chinese. Shortly before the above-mentioned events, a funeral was held in Guangdong Province for a well-known "aunty" who had been one of the most respected Bible distributors in the country. A Back to Jerusalem International worker was asked to come and share a few words, but when it was observed that Pastor Dennis Balcombe had arrived, he respectfully declined and quietly gave his condolences to the daughter of the deceased.

Joshua, one of the second-tier leaders from the Five Brothers Network asked the coworker why he declined speaking, but quickly understood the situation. He looked out over the crowd and saw Pastor Balcombe's friendly face greeting people as he entered the back room. Joshua also declined meeting with him.

Joshua had nothing but love and gratefulness for all that Balcombe had done for China and Henan Province, but rumors had started to spread that he was traveling on an official visa to China and working together with the official church. Joshua told the Back to Jerusalem worker that Pastor Balcombe was encouraging house churches to think about taking the step to register. It was something that his leadership could not fathom at that time. Though not aware of any of Pastor Balcombe's efforts, the foreign coworker could see that Joshua was conflicted.

Because of the betrayal that many believers felt from the first leaders of the official church in China—those in Henan especially—there is a deep chasm between the House Church and official church today. Memories of past betrayals keep House Church leaders weary of doing anything with their official counterparts. Today there are many foreigners who would like to work with the Chinese church in an official manner so if they cannot work with the underground House Church they are willing to work with the official church and walk the line dictated by the government.

Peter Xu set a standard of unity with fellow House Church believers in China, but refused to bow to pressure from the government to join a movement that underground believers felt to be both immoral and treacherous. The unity started with the Sinim Fellowship continues to this day.

Today many people ask, "What has happened to the Sinim Fellowship? It was such a huge thing in the late 1990s and early 2000s, but we haven't heard anything about it lately."

The Sinim Fellowship served its purpose by uniting the churches in China. What God spoke to Peter Xu set the stage for the unified work that is taking place in China today. It is true that there are many fellowships and networks that do not actively work together in China. The Sinim Fellowship did not create a utopia of happiness and eternal bliss, nor did it solve all of the problems of personal differences between the major House Church networks. Today there are leaders who will not hold meetings on the same day in the same city for fear that they might brush shoulders with each other. However, what the Sinim Fellowship did do is unite the underground House Church against the foreign denominations that attempted to control the revival in China with their own set of ideologies. It also unified the church against a government that attempted to impose its own atheistic-flavored ideology on the House Church.

Today, even though some of the large networks will not work directly with one another, they will also not actively persecute one another or attempt to make publications ridiculing one another. This can mainly be attributed to the impact of unity established by the Sinim Fellowship.

Eventually the Sinim Fellowship continued in theory, but not in practice. With five rebel leaders who were always either on the run or in prison, there was no possible way for the Sinim Fellowship to survive long term.

Brother Yun and his family miraculously escaped China and found asylum in Europe. Peter Xu also left China and sought asylum in the US, where he now works closely with his sister. Pastor Wang ended up back in prison. Zhang Rongliang went to prison for making numerous trips abroad on falsified travel documents. Pastor Shen was then left to have meetings all by himself, but that couldn't be considered an actual fellowship.

Most of the information about the Born Again Movement's current situation is contradictory and incomplete. One reason for this is Peter Xu's extended physical absence from China. Xu was a very strong and involved leader, so in his absence a lot has changed. Peter can give information regarding his church in China, but without having been there in many years his own idea of the current situation is vague and incomplete. China has changed greatly since he left and it is not easy to imagine the new guidelines that are being used by the current House Church.

Without Peter Xu, the church has indeed fragmented into smaller groups. These fragmented groups are made up of new faces and young ambitious leaders. Many of the leaders from the new generation have never met with Peter Xu and are not familiar with the way things used to be.

These days Peter Xu is also focused on working with other churches around the world to connect them with his partners in China. His role has changed from leader to ambassador. It has not been easy for him to leave his role as leader of one of China's largest House Church networks. It wasn't his preference to live in exile and if given the chance to return to his coworkers in China it is almost certain that he would be on the next plane.

With the new wave of underground churches in China, there is a new phase of independence that is sweeping throughout the country. These new churches are more modern, more mobile, and a lot more independent. As China grows, these churches are growing with it. Underground House Church networks that are massive and controlled by one single leader like the Born Again Movement under Peter Xu are becoming a thing of the past.

The underground House Church networks that are in place in China today are adapting and continuing to operate, but the chances of a new network developing and growing into several million believers are not as high under the current conditions. In many ways that is a good thing, because it indicates a couple of exciting developments:

1. The Chinese people have more gospel resources than ever before. In the past, God worked through just a handful of people to share the gospel with many, but today God is using lots of people to reach many more.

2. The church growth is taking place in more urban settings. Urban areas in China tend to be more transient with new workers and residents coming and going all the time. By contrast, rural areas where the underground house churches initially exploded were made up of closely-knit communities where families had been living for generations. People in these rural communities were loyal to each other when they were animists, and they remained loyal to each other as believers in Christ. Today these rural communities are made up of mainly children and the elderly, while most of the young adults have left for the urban areas to make money.

It is yet to be seen how these two factors will change the methods and practices of the Chinese House Church networks, but they will inevitably adapt as the Spirit leads.

13

TRUTH HOUSE CHURCH NETWORK

Truth Network is one of the networks more shrouded in mystery than any other network in China. Very little information is available about its history, founder, leadership, or activities. This chapter will give a brief introduction to this underground network that very few people around the world—including those familiar with China—know anything about. Though it is not as famous as the Henan networks or even as well-known as its Anhui counterpart—Blessing Network, the Truth Network is one of the most important underground House Church networks in China and will play a major role in determining the future of the House Church.

If the Truth Network were an individual, she would be tagged the strong silent type. Truth does not make much noise or garner much public attention, but without a doubt this network is making the largest impact for world missions today if measured by the amount of money spent or the number of missionaries sent out from China.

More than likely, some donor organizations around the world that consider themselves experts on the House Church in China will disagree with some of the information laid out in this chapter. Many so-called China experts have come to the conclusion years ago that the Henan networks are the largest in China and their assumptions can be verified on major websites like Wikipedia. However, we would once again like to caution the reader that virtually everything related to China is constantly changing. What was true in the year 2000 is not necessarily true twelve years later. Many experts today still rely on studies that were conducted more than fifteen years ago. These studies are outdated and need to be replaced by new ones in order to get the facts as they are—not as they used to be. All statistical reports coming out of China are limited because of the political situation and all facts are based on the range of exposure. Exposure is limited to every organization working in China and those with maximum exposure provide very few (if any) reports. Any report that comes out of China, including the information given in this book, needs to be evaluated based on the amount, duration, and dates of exposure the researchers have had. Keeping those factors in mind will help evaluate the situation of the Chinese House Church.

Truth will be the last large network covered in this book. The five most famous networks have traditionally been Tanghe (China Gospel Fellowship), Nanyang (Born Again Movement), Fangcheng (China for Christ), Lixin (Blessing), and Yingshan (Truth).

Born Again was thought to be the largest at one time, but things changed when Peter Xu left China. Fangcheng is thought by many to be the largest House Church in China, but that is not accounting for the splitting-off of the Five Brothers Network. Tanghe is the likely choice as the largest church in China today and is often thought of as such. However, there is information about this amazing church in Anhui, the Truth Network, that few people are aware of.

Truth has continued to grow exponentially and for the last few years has been producing more missionaries and evangelists than any other network in China. In 2011, Truth had more than sixty Bible schools throughout China and every year they graduate more than 1,500 evangelists and missionaries. This does not include their pastoral, Sunday school teacher, and grassroots worker training programs.

The 1,500 evangelists are supported and organized through the network and strategically sent out to different areas with needs. They send out missionaries in groups of ten to twenty-five at a time and the network has appointed two mission directors to oversee the implementation of the missions work. These two mission directors are supplied with almost US$200,000 per year entirely from the house churches, not foreigners.

Two hundred thousand dollars may not sound like a lot of money compared to large mission organizations in the western world, but Truth Network is based in rural Anhui Province and most of their network is made up of poor farmers. This means that they do not have any large headquarters or buildings to pay for every month. This US$200,000 also does not include the outside resources and funding that they receive in support from foreign organizations, which is much more than the amount that they are able to raise in house. This amount of resources shows how important world missions is to Truth Network. This dogged and determined focus is just one of the factors that have contributed to their growth in China and abroad.

Today Truth Network has more missionaries on the field than any other network in China. It is even possible to say that Truth had more missionaries on the field in 2011 than all the other networks in China combined.

In our almost twelve years of working with Truth, we have met with the leadership on a regular basis, but have never asked about their history or background until one night in February of 2012 while gathering research for this book. We spend most of our time working with the lower leadership of Truth, so it was exciting to meet with their senior leader, Pastor Chen, in Shanghai. He is a stout man with a comb-over and strong round facial features. We began talking about the projects that we had completed together in 2011 and the vision for 2012.

After discussing all of our projects together the author asked him to provide a brief history of the church for this book. He was caught off guard and obviously had not been asked that question often, but once he got started, he continued telling stories about the early church and the founding of the Truth Network for over two hours.

As we munched on mandarin oranges, China's main winter fruit, Pastor Chen talked about the political situation in the early days, which was basically the same for all the other networks. "After the 1960s," he began, "It was not easy for any of the Christians left in China. They relied a lot on the foreign missionaries. The foreigners read the Bible for them. They preached for them, led the churches, and led the prayers. When the foreigners left, the old Christians were not sure of anything. They didn't know how to pray. They didn't have a strong understanding of the Bible. They only knew that Jesus was God."

Unlike Henan Province where there were strong personalities that can be traced back in history, the history of the church in Anhui is not as straightforward. The Truth Network cannot be traced back to the work and efforts of one man or missionary.

In Henan Province there were giants of the faith like

149

Jonathan Goforth, Marie Monsen, Li Tainen, etc., but the same cannot be said of Anhui. Undoubtedly there were key players who cultivated the land in Anhui, but the imprint is not as strong or as traceable.

"I cannot really point to one person who really came and shared the gospel with us," Pastor Chen recalls. Even though he was clearly well-versed in Chinese history and church history in China, he was not able to point to a central figure that ignited the fire of church growth in Anhui. "During the days of Mao Zedong, my village area was one of the poorest in China. The villagers went mad. They were demon possessed. We didn't know it then, but there were entire villages that were possessed by demons."

The villages in and around Yinshang County had so many people that were completely out of their minds because they had lost all hope. There were no hospitals to go to for diagnoses and there was no money to pay for any treatment even if the diagnoses were clear. Pastor Chen was born in 1956 and raised in Yinshang County during the darkest years of Chinese history. His family lived close to the banks of the Huai River and had experienced their share of hardships. His family had a history of cancer and deafness. His grandfather went deaf at an early age and died of cancer. His father went completely deaf and died of cancer at the age of thirty-one.

> When I was younger I realized that I too was going deaf. In 1979 I was almost completely deaf in both ears and was showing the signs of early cancer. I was sick and too weak to move. I knew that my time on earth was not going to last much longer. One of my in-laws came and shared the gospel with me and it was at that time that I accepted Jesus as my Lord. On that day I was completely healed. No one could explain it. We didn't know how it worked. We only knew that it was the name of Jesus that healed me.

> That is how the church grew in Yinshang in the early days. Those ten years between 1980 and 1990 were full of revival throughout that area. The biggest attraction was the casting out of demons. People were bringing to the Christians their demon-possessed family members who were out of control and the demons would immediately leave.

In Yinshang, ancestoral worship and tormenting from

demons is a deeply-rooted cultural practice. Fengshui is based on this idea of creating good *qi* so that all forces flow naturally without stopping the flow of dragons or demons. The positioning of wind chimes and mirrors is very important in the Fengshui practiced in Anhui. Houses, rooms, and all other structures were built in ways deemed non-offensive to demons. The lives of the people were focused on appeasing the demons so that they would not torment the family.

Demon possession may not be a common visible occurrence in the western world, but in China it was very real and dictated every aspect of life. Even today in Hong Kong it is a deeply-held belief and no one will dare offend the demons and risk getting bad luck. Millions of dollars are spent by large western companies to hire experts to create an auspicious environment that does not offend the demons. Fengshui is adopted and implemented in places like Hong Kong Disneyland and dragon dancers are hired to scare away the evil spirits at upscale shopping malls throughout the city.

> So many people were being set free from demons that there was no doubt about the power of the name of Jesus. We didn't know how to pray. We didn't have a Bible. We didn't know anything except what the old Christians told us regarding crying out in the name of Jesus.
>
> During the 1980s to 1990s there wasn't a farmer left in the field on Sunday. Everyone flocked to the name of Jesus.Our village went from a village with no believers to a village where everyone was a believer. Even today if you travel to Yingshan County you will find that almost everyone you meet is a believer in Jesus Christ.

Like the other networks that were discussed in the earlier chapters, the revivals in Yingshang County did not start off with the purpose of being a large movement. It was just the natural flow of the power of the Holy Spirit. The Truth Network is mostly referred to by the county where it started, Yingshan.

"I can't really say that there was a defining moment where we began to adopt the name 'Truth' as the name of our network. Maybe I wasn't even there, but the best that I can remember was that there was a pastor from Taiwan who was arranging a large meeting in the mid-nineties. He asked us what the name of our group was. We didn't know. We just referred to people that came from our county as Yingshan. The pastor told us that we needed a name that we could use to register, so we used 'Truth.' I mean, we believe in the truth of Jesus Christ, so it sounded natural to me."

The churches grew rapidly during the 1980s, especially where those like Pastor Chen had seen the miracles of God performed in their midst. The villagers were too poor to buy medicine or see a doctor when they were sick, so their only hope was the prayers of the Christians. They were not disappointed. Many people were healed and had their lives transformed, never to be the same again.

> Our church continued to grow. Every time I was arrested, I saw the Lord blessing the church of Yingshan more and more. In 2003 I was arrested and the arresting officer told me that I was one of the most wanted men in all of China. Out of all the criminals in China I was among the top six in all of eastern China.
>
> Even though the government sought to destroy us and stomp out our church, they were not able to. Even if you go to the Three-Self government church in our area, you will quickly understand that they are the minority. The unbelievers and the official church in Yingshan are the minority group. Our House Church makes up most of the population.

Today Truth has stepped onto a new frontier in China. They are not registered, but they are recognized and respected by the local police and officials. Truth has started an officially-recognized school that provides education for children from kindergarten all the way through high school.

Upon learning about the school, some locals were concerned and immediately began their attempts to sabotage the efforts. "They didn't want us to have a school that taught children," Pastor Chen said. "The government immediately had problems with the facility and said that it didn't meet their standards, but I knew that it was more than that so I called up the officials. I asked them if we were being stopped just because we were Christians. The official emphatically denied that they were trying to stop anything. Eventually, we got our school up and running and today we have more than one thousand students, not including kindergarteners."

Pastor Chen has come a long way since being the sixth most wanted criminal in all of eastern China. Today Pastor Chen has missionaries in many different countries, such as Ethiopia, Pakistan, Cambodia, Myanmar, Nepal, Uzbekistan, Laos, and at the time of writing he has ten students currently at the Back to Jerusalem training facility in the Philippines.

Truth also has students that are attending universities around the world to equip them with the tools that they need to train others for the future. They are in prestigious universities like Oxford and Cambridge and are dedicated to returning to China and using their skills to aid the Back to Jerusalem movement.

When asked what the greatest need is for Truth, without hesitation Pastor Chen replied, "Bibles! We still have a huge Bible deficit everywhere we go."

Pastor Chen has a passion to get the Bible and other teaching resources into the hands of believers. In 2011 we received the following testimony from a young believer named Brother En who had been directly handed a Bible by Pastor Chen:

Brother En

I had my back to the wall and there was no hope in my life. It was at that time that I received a Bible from Uncle Chen (Pastor Chen). He said to me, "If you want hope in your life, read this." That night I started to read the Bible that he gave me. I read it all night long. When I read in Matthew 8:17, "He took our illnesses and bore our diseases," I began to weep. I cried so loudly that it woke up my family. They came to me asking why I was crying. I could not say anything. I could not stop crying. Instead of asking more questions, they just joined me and began to cry as well.

Before I was a Christian, I had a disease in my throat that prevented me from eating normally, but after that day I was completely healed. The next morning I

153

woke up and brushed my teeth and sat down to eat real food. I had been completely healed. Hallelujah! My family could not believe their eyes. As soon as they saw that I was healed, they immediately began to believe in Jesus and they too became Christians.

Thank you for sending the Bible to me. May God bless you in every situation. I ask God to bless your team (the Back to Jerusalem team).

Here is another letter given to us from Truth Network after delivering Bibles to Brother Hua:

Brother Hua

Dear Brothers in the Lord:

Peace to you!

The reason I am writing this letter is because we have seen so many people blessed by your support. Today there are 236 believers in our church, and they all now have their own Bible! We have Bible studies every evening and morning together. How precious His Word is to us! In Ps 119:11, it says, "I have stored up your word in my heart, that I might not sin against you." I have seen most of the people at our Bible study have their lives completely changed. Today there are many believers that are praying with us that used to be thieves, liars, and gamblers. Some of them would fight with anyone and everyone at every opportunity. All of us are new in Christ and have been changed forever.

We have had several women in our group that could not give birth to children, but after coming to the cross and following Jesus they were able to get pregnant and have a baby. There are so many testimonies in our small group that I could write all day. I just want to say thank you for your gift and because of your support we have seen an incredible increase in believers. We have many testimonies and new believers here. God bless you!

The collaborative delivery of Bibles between Truth Network and Back to Jerusalem International is amazing. We sometimes receive letters from the network that actually show that people became Christians when they received a Bible, like this letter from Sister Han:

Sister Han

First I give thanks to our God! Thank you for supporting our church for all of these years. I remember when I received my first Bible. It was provided by you. When I first received it, I didn't know what it was and what the book was about. I thought that it must be a history book or a biography. After I read it and studied it I gave my heart to Christ. Because of your contribution, I was able to obtain life as well as strength and courage to minister to others.

Truth Network continues to break barriers in China. Like the other underground House Church networks, they are delivering Bibles as quickly as they can. There has been a direct relationship between the delivery of Bibles and the growth of the church in China. The Back to Jerusalem website (*backtojerusalem.com*) and Facebook page are regularly updated with stories and testimonies of Bibles that are delivered in China.

14

MISSIONARY TRAINING

It was well past sunset when the cargo ship's gangplank dropped on a remote island in the Philippines. Waves gently crashed against the old ship's hull as a former US Marine stepped onto the dock. He waded his way through the sea of industrial vehicles also exiting the boat and hopped in the back of a small container truck. He was on his way to a Chinese House Church missionary training center where he was going to put the students through the ringer. These missionary students, who had been training for months in the Philippines, were in for a long night and they had no idea what was coming.

Another mystery to be uncovered about the Chinese House Church is their method of training. Several years ago many western churchgoers were alarmed to hear from people like Brother Yun that Chinese missionaries were being taught how to get out of handcuffs or jump out of windows to escape the police. Such statements made it sound like Chinese missionaries were more like secret agents and fugitives than emissaries of the gospel. This misunderstanding underscores the striking difference between western and Chinese House Church missionary training.

This became a problem while setting up the Back to Jerusalem Foundation in the United Kingdom. Our first application was rejected after government officials read the introductory material about our organization. It seemed that the UK government was not interested in registering a charity organization that taught missionaries how to break out of handcuffs, jump from moving vehicles, and escape from prison. Those registration papers were later modified to the liking of the UK government so we could register.

Very little about Chinese House Church training resembles anything in the West. Chinese Bible schools do not take place on campuses with beautiful manicured lawns, quaint chapels, and administration buildings. Graduations are not celebrated with smiling parents taking pictures and waving obnoxious banners. Deans in colored gowns are not present to give long drawn-out speeches with the occasional interruption of well-rehearsed jokes.

In China, Bible schools often take place in small simple apartments, located in dingy high-rise buildings towering over overpopulated townships covered in coal dust. An apartment as small as six hundred square feet (almost fifty-six square meters) may be used for a Bible school with as many as thirty students. To keep the neighbors from growing suspicious, the students move in and stay in the apartment for months at a time without leaving. Usually one person will be assigned the job of going out to purchase food and supplies. Occasionally a teacher might be seen coming and going, but the students will remain as stationary as possible.

Every window will be covered and no door will be opened before checking out the peephole to make sure that the visitor is not the local police or a curious neighbor. Though most Chinese house churches are charismatic, they will muffle their prayers and sing at almost whisper volume to keep their voices from being heard outside.

The first Bible schools were held in countryside churches, but that changed as China opened up and it became possible to travel to major cities. The cities became choice locations for Bible schools because such gatherings are not as likely to be noticed in a noisy city. Quite recently, however, the need for vocational training for missionaries has caused many Bible schools and missionary training centers to start moving back to the rural areas.

Rural areas allow for lower overhead expenses as well as the space needed for vocational training; especially training that involves agriculture. There was a brief period of time when rural training sites were becoming scarce, but today there is a considerable rise among them. Other benefits of rural training are that security can be monitored a lot more easily and activities are not as easily noticed. The downside is that routes to and from the rural training areas can very easily be monitored by the authorities.

The Back to Jerusalem school in the Philippines is not a typical missionary training center. It was selected as a place to give Chinese missionaries exposure to serving in a foreign land. It gives the Chinese a chance to work in a country that has a different culture, language, and history. The Philippines is an ideal location for training missionaries because it is a Catholic country open for preaching the gospel. In the Philippines Chinese missionaries have the opportunity to work with militant Muslims, Buddhists, Atheists, and Animists. It is unique to find a place where there is freedom to share the Good News with such a variety of religions.

The other benefit of training in the Philippines is that most educated people there speak English, which is the primary foreign language the missionaries are taught at training centers in China. Although the missionaries may be trained in other languages as well, English is quite often their first foreign language. The Philippines is one of the few places within easy traveling distance from China where Chinese are able to work with the locals using English as the common language.

Like most other Back to Jerusalem training centers, the facility in the Philippines is very atypical. The concept is based on the first century church. Students are given a strong practical mission focus that includes a brief introduction of the local minority mountain tribes, some practical guidelines, and hands-on evangelism experience in those areas. The Chinese live in the villages, preach the gospel, and work with the locals for a week or more before returning to the classroom. Upon their return they discuss what they did, saw, and experienced. The students discuss which strategies worked and which ones did not and are then sent back to the "bush" to minister to the same villagers a week later.

There is an undeniable tendency in our age for those with more theological training to be less evangelistic. It seems like the more theological degrees a person has the more likely they are to spend their time debating nuances with other believers instead of reaching lost sinners. With training that focuses on hands-on evangelism rather than sitting in a classroom, Back to Jerusalem missionaries are able to maintain their emphasis on the people they are ministering to and not on theological debates.

The following depicts another aspect of Chinese missionary training that may be controversial in the West. The former Marine we left in the back of a container truck recounts his mission:

> As we drove down the narrow island road, the evening breeze was coming through the windows. The mountains were silhouetted in the moonlight. We pulled up to the

first guard check point. The guards knew the friends I was traveling with well. They knew we were on our way to meet a couple of their colleagues who had worked with the police department in the past.

Their colleagues were going to help me with the interrogation. The students knew me, but they had never met these former policemen. After meeting with the former policemen and going over the interrogation schedule with them, it was time to start waking up the students to be interrogated.

None of their leaders in China were even told about this training for fear that it would compromise the element of surprise. None of the curriculum even alluded to the fact that tonight they would be put through a surprise interrogation. They wouldn't even know that it was only training!

Having a background in special operations from the US military and making the training curriculum with a friend with US Army Special Forces experience allowed for a unique program.

Around midnight we sent for the first person to be interrogated. One of the English teachers went into the dorm room and woke up a brother.

"Wake up. The police are here and for some reason they want to speak with you," he said as the student was waking up.

The first student to be interrogated was taken to a separate location where the police were waiting. They were very friendly and welcomed the student into the interrogation room. We had secret cameras set up that allowed us to film the entire event.

"Sorry to wake you up and disturb you," the first officer said as they shook hands and he directed the student over to a chair.

"We just have a few really quick questions and then you can go back to bed." The Chinese student was visibly nervous.

"Can you tell me about the nature of your training here?"

"I am here for language training. I am studying

English."

One of the officers spoke in a low, calm, friendly voice and the other officer strategically remained quiet for the perfect "good cop, bad cop" tactic.

I viewed the entire interrogation from another room and closely monitored the situation for the best way to move forward to extract information from the student. Every five minutes one of the officers would leave the room and I would hand him a piece of paper with the next line of questions.

The first questions were mainly to allow the students to incriminate themselves. We let the students talk about how they were learning the English language and the reasons why they chose to study in the Philippines. We encouraged them to talk about things that they didn't need to talk about and fueled small talk.

Every time I gave the police a new batch of questions, they were progressively more intrusive and within an hour we began to have our first contradiction. We noted it for future reference and moved on. We then had our next contradiction, made a note, and moved on.

Soon we had a circle of stories that were exploitable and it was time for us to pounce. I began to tell the interrogators to ask about Back to Jerusalem.

"What do you know about Back to Jerusalem?" The interrogator asked.

"I hear it's a beautiful city," the student replied. I had to keep myself from laughing. It was such a great stall technique by the student.

"No, it is a Chinese movement to go into other countries and subvert the population through religious and ideological teaching. Isn't that right?"

I signaled for one of the officers to come out so I could coach him to go harder after the student. When he exited the room and shut the door, I put my hand on his shoulder, looked into his eyes, and told him to close the space.

"For the last hour I have told you to get progressively closer to the student. I wanted him to feel his space being invaded by you as your questions became progressively more intrusive. Now I want you to be up in his face. I want him to feel threatened. I want you to threaten his safety. Take away his feeling of security."

I didn't realize that my idea of threatening and his idea were two different things! He stormed back into the room, got up in the students face and maintained strong eye contact.

"You need to start telling me what I want to know or I am going to stab you and then cut your throat!"

"Yikes!" I frantically began to wave for the interrogator to come back out into the hallway. I started to have misgivings that this entire interrogation could go very wrong. After more time had passed I began to hand the interrogators pictures of the students' leaders back in China. We also presented them with flight schedules to Muslim areas where they had flown earlier to share the gospel. At the very end, the interrogators presented a picture of me.

"Do you know this man," they asked. "I am Chinese. Is he Chinese?" the student asked.

"No, he is American."

"How would I know an American? I am Chinese," the student quickly shot back.

The interrogators questioned the student over and over about information on me until finally I walked into the room. When I entered the room it was already several hours into the morning and we had been conducting the interrogation all night. I greeted them with a friendly "*Ni hao*" and explained everything.

"This has all been a test. Training. These guys are our friends and are not real police."

One of the students was a quiet young lady. She was one of the youngest in the entire group and was as thin as a twig. When the students first arrived in Hong Kong, I asked them to stay for one week so that I could get them prepared for the training in the Philippines.

We would often hike up the mountain behind Hong Kong International Airport, pray together in the mountains, and have communion together. This young lady literally had to be carried up the last part of the hike.

She was so weak and lacked energy. She was used to being in the city dorms all day and not accustomed to much physical exercise.

I assumed that she would be the easiest person to crack. Getting her to break down would make the night go much faster. It would have also been great to have her reaction on camera so that we could later show the tapes to the rest of the class and talk about what to do and not do.

She was woken up in a separate living area and brought into the interrogation room. I don't know how she saw the cameras so fast, but she did and immediately sat in the interrogators chair. The two interrogators were being nice and polite and asked her to sit in the other chair.

"Thank you," she said politely. "I am fine."

"No, you need to sit here," they insisted.

"Thank you so much, but I am fine." She stood up and led the interrogators by the hand to sit. They followed her instructions!

I could not believe my eyes. This young lady who seemed to be as timid as a mouse had just fooled our guys into siting exactly where she wanted them to.

The interrogators began with their line of instructed questioning. As the questions got more intense, she began to make signals of having to go to the bathroom.

"Can I go to the restroom," she asked.

The interrogators came out and told me that the student needed to go to the restroom. "No. We need to use this to our advantage. Tell her that she cannot use the restroom until she answers all of our questions. Maybe that will expedite the process."

As night turned into morning, it was clear that she was smarter than all of us. She took every question and turned it around on the interrogators and did it in the nicest, sweetest way. Her sweet words and demeanor masked her clever tenacity.

I ended the interrogation prematurely. It was not going our way. After I finally ended it and told her that it was only training I then offered her a chance to use the toilet.

"I don't have to use the toilet," she said softly.

"I just made that up so that I could make a run for it."

We called it a night and then the following day we began teaching about interrogation. One of the underground church pastors from China came to assist me. I talked about methodology and techniques and he talked about his experiences. This pastor had been arrested several times and had been interrogated in China on many occasions. He talked about the different ways he was interrogated, what the police were looking for, and the different ways that he was able deflect their questions for short periods of time.

Many westerners may find this kind of training a bit overboard and unnecessary, but the truth is that many Chinese have never been outside of China. They get nervous when going through immigration checkpoints. We needed to prepare them for at least the basic questioning used at immigration.

Although we would never do these things, we taught the students that in areas where interrogation is not developed, beatings and physical abuse usually serve as the primary means of interrogation. We explained that outside of clever questioning, the other means of breaking down barriers are food deprivation, sleep deprivation, beatings, family manipulation, isolation, long-term discomfort, and pain infliction without markings.

I told them, "When going through interrogation or immigration you have to adopt a personality different than the one you have now. Before God you are used to admitting your guilt and asking for forgiveness. Your guilt is assumed and you come before God asking Him to forgive you, but to be forgiven you have to admit your sins. This attitude needs to be left at the door during interrogation. Remain emotionless at immigration and interrogation. Most hardened criminals do not have guilt and believe in themselves. Practical interrogation manuals are generally based on the extensive experience of interrogators and offer allegedly-effective techniques for breaking down a suspect's resistance."

The main point of our interrogation class was,

"Don't give up information easily and never lie. Make yourself like an onion. Make the interrogators peel off each layer."

"Forget your guilt. If you want to be successfully interviewed and walk away clean you have to remain guiltless," I taught. "You have to say to yourself, 'I didn't do anything wrong. I didn't say anything wrong. You are wrong. You are at fault. This has nothing to do with me.' Watch your body language. Move as little as possible and be disciplined. Occupy your thoughts with something else. Don't think about the situation unless you are preparing your story."

"Rule number one that you must never forget is *never* lie. Just don't tell the whole truth. Your story never has to change. You don't have to lie; you just don't have to tell them the whole truth."

At this course we teach about the "good cop, bad cop" technique as well. We also taught maximization technique which is based on imposing maximum fear for not cooperating. We also taught about the use of undercover informants, which was one of the tactics used by the Eastern Lightning in China when attempting to convert the Tanghe leadership.

"A plain clothed officer is one of the best ways to get information," I said. "Whether in prison, secondary immigration, or even in your daily activities, this method can give a lot of information to people who interview you so they can give you the illusion that they know everything. The interrogation takes place during conversations without your knowledge. Even if they already know everything, make them work for it. Make them work for every piece of information. Don't give up anything for free. Don't get cocky. You don't do this for a living. Your best policy is to *shut up*. Keep your mouth *shut*. Silence is the best policy, above all else. Silence is the best policy. Don't talk with your mouth and don't talk with your body."

"Deflect! Deflect! Deflect! You have no rights when being interrogated. If you do, they will try to tell you early on, and they will not repeat any rights you might have. When they tell you – you probability will not be aware of it. Always insist on talking to someone else at every turn. Say you want an attorney of your choice, or to talk to your family. The best way to get out of guilt is deflection. Deflect to the guilt of your interrogators and to talking to someone else!"

We taught the students about behavioral observation and different techniques to discipline the body from giving away information that interrogators are looking for.

"Micro-expressions lasting less than one-fifth of a second may leak emotions someone wants to conceal, such as anger or guilt. At the same time, signs of emotion aren't necessarily signs of guilt. An innocent person may be apprehensive and appear guilty, but don't be that person. Take control of your body and voice. Learn techniques that work for you."

Although some might find it excessive, this type of interrogation training is the best way we have found so far to help prepare underground Back to Jerusalem missionaries for countries that aggressively oppose proselytizing. It is just one of the many ways that underground House Church missionaries differ from their western counterparts.

15

LIXIN HOUSE CHURCH NETWORK

The Churches in Anhui Province are not as well-known as those in Henan. Very few people know anything about them, let alone their historical background. Despite our organization having served the churches in Anhui for over a decade, we still know little about their history. We know their leaders and are familiar with their current projects, overall vision, and how they operate on a day-to-day basis, but our meetings with them are focused on working out the nuts and bolts projects, rather than racking their brains for stories.

We support their evangelists, missionaries, and Bibles for distribution, and have also been helping their Bible schools for years, but still somehow rarely seem to find the time to share a meal with their top leaders. Even on those rare occasions we never talk about things like church history.

No one really talks about the history of the underground House Church in China. This is a tragedy because a new generation of Chinese Christians is growing up with no knowledge of their own spiritual roots. In the West we can walk into any Christian bookstore and buy plenty of books about Martin Luther, John Wycliffe, Jonathan Edwards, or church history in general. Westerners can purchase online vast volumes on church history that could take several lifetimes to read, but in China there is virtually nothing about their churches. There are countless stories of martyrs and immense sacrifice that will never be told.

Westerners have more historical information regarding the Chinese House Church than its own members do. Informative books like *Jesus in Beijing*, *Back to Jerusalem*, or *The Heavenly Man* are simply not available for purchase in China. Even this book will undoubtedly be unavailable in China.

Apart from security reasons, Chinese Christians just do

not have the time to sit around and talk about the amazing works of God they have witnessed. The leadership of Lixin Network has never approached anyone with a glossy full-color brochure that talks about their church of five million believers. They wouldn't even think of mentioning that they are one of the five largest House Church networks in China, nor that they are one of the largest movements in all of Anhui Province with more congregants than the entire nation of Norway.

With all that said, it actually took much prodding to get the information from this chapter out of Lixin's leaders. It was largely extracted from a report they gave us on Bible distribution in June of 2011. Back to Jerusalem usually connects with them twice a year to talk about Bible delivery with their network.

The story leading up to the meeting is quite typical of ministry life in China. The leader was coming from a training session for workers from ten different provinces. He almost didn't make it out of the session. On the second day of teaching there was a teacher who no one had ever seen before. He ended up being an undercover policeman who had infiltrated the meeting. No one is sure how it happened. The meeting was raided by the local police the following day, but the leader had left just before the raid.

The police burst into the meeting and detained all of the leaders. Every one of them was detained, questioned, and had their names recorded in the local log book to document their unregistered meeting and illegal activities before being released.

What's important to realize is that this raid did not take place during the Cultural Revolution of the 1970s, but in June of 2011. There is still a very real persecution taking place on a regular basis in China and most of it goes unnoticed because there are many foreign organizations and nations that turn a blind eye to it in order to maintain a good relationship with China.

Several years before that, in another meeting that included representatives from Lixin, a group of foreign supporters of the Chinese House Church got to have a small taste of the real situation in China. While the historic meeting was underway, a large group of uniformed police came down the hotel's spiral staircase towards the room we were meeting in. A local Chinese brother who had worked with the police department in the past noticed them and alerted the Chinese leaders at the meeting. Those leaders immediately exited out the side door opposite where the police were and quickly blended into the crowd on the street, while most of the westerners waited to see what would happen. One woman in the back of the room panicked and started to become hysterical.

When the police walked down the staircase towards our meeting they quickly turned aside and went directly to the massage parlor. The conference room just happened to be directly adjacent to a Chinese spa. Even though it was a false alarm, for a brief moment several foreigner Christians felt what it is like to be a Chinese in a normal prayer meeting. For just a few seconds those westerners were able to relate in a very small way with what most Chinese go through every time they meet for worship.

At about nine in the evening after the raided training session, the leader from Lixin Church arrived at our hotel and almost immediately we began to discuss the need for Bibles in China. We had provided tens of thousands of Bibles for Lixin House Church in the past so they wanted to discuss the future need. After talking about the projects as usual, we intentionally steered the conversation toward the history of the network. The situation was awkward at first and all the leaders in the room knew that it was a strange request, but they graciously gave us a brief history of their network. Enguan, the founder of Lixin Network, sat back on the couch and was so taken off guard that he had to pause a moment to organize his thoughts.

Lixin, originally named after Lixin County, is also known as "Blessing" or "Mongfu" in Chinese. Many of the Henan networks have tried to move past the county names they were branded with, but old habits die hard. We usually refer to the county name when speaking with members of Tanghe or Fangcheng, but with Lixin we almost always call them Mongfu.

Enguan was saved in 1978 and immediately began to preach the gospel in his area. He established Lixin Network in 1985 in Anhui Province's Lixin County. In 1994, Enguan tried to estimate the number of people in his church and he estimated the number to be about three million believers at the time. The network has continued to grow drastically, so it has not been easy to estimate how many people now belong to it. Those who know about the areas Lixin is working in and how many leaders they have in those areas would estimate the numbers to be between five and seven million believers at the time of writing.

Like the other House Church networks that we have

discussed before, Enguan never assumed that the small underground House Church gatherings that took place in the middle of the night would ever grow to anything other than just a few saints coming together to sing praises to their King. They never dreamed that their small meetings would grow outside of their backward poor rural region of Lixin County.

"Since the founding of the church in 1985 in Lixin, we have seen the number of people coming to the Lord every year grow and grow. There is no way we can possibly keep count," Enguan said when trying to remember the early years.

Enguan was sixteen years old when he was saved. At the age of fourteen his father became ill and soon died. Two years later his mother also came down with a serious illness. She had also been demon possessed for a long time. His older brother had serious issues with his ears, but his family was too poor to pay for treatment. The family had not had the money to help his father when he became sick two years earlier and still did not have money to help his mother or brother.

"I believe that God used poverty to teach me to trust in Him," he said as a matter of fact.

There were six Christians who lived in his village at that time. None of them were educated nor could they read. His uncle was one of those six Christians. He would often sing old hymns to his God, but did not have a Bible or any significant formal education. Even though Enguan was not a Christian, he was comforted during those most trying times by hearing his uncle's songs. He asked his uncle to teach him the old hymns that he was always singing. Once he learned them he found comfort in their words and peace in their melodies. Before he was even a Christian, he would share the hymns with others. He could see how God was even using him even though he was not yet a believer.

He wanted to ask the Christians to come and pray for his mother because of her demon possession, but in China it is customary to feed houseguests. He didn't have any food to give them if they came to his home to pray for his mother. Since they couldn't afford rice flour, eventually he made flour out of sweet potatoes and offered it to the Christians in his village when they came over to pray.

During their visits he would listen carefully to every word that they prayed. Since he couldn't afford to keep asking them to come and pray for his mother, he memorized the words of their prayers and prayed them over her himself.

One day he knelt down and began praying for his mother and suddenly she was healed and set free from demon possession. All of the local Christians who heard about it rejoiced. At that time the local Christians didn't have any worship services, so Enguan began to hold meetings at his home, which became the very first House Church of Lixin County. The formation of Lixin House Church Network had begun.

There were other families in the area that also had members who were completely out of their minds with unexplainable madness. Word began to get around that this kind of uncontrollable behavior could be demon possession. Enguan began to get requests to travel around and pray for those who were demon possessed. When he prayed, people would be set free from the demons and entire families came to the Lord.

Enguan did not have a Bible, thus he had no way to reference any of the prayers he was praying, nor any way to formally introduce people to the God who was setting them free from demon possession. To him Jesus was only a name that demonstrated power of deliverance and he placed his faith in the name of Jesus.

All he knew were the old hymns taught him by the old believers in the village. Whenever there were people that needed prayer he would pray the few words that he had heard prayed before in the name of Jesus and sing the hymns. People were set free and he began to see miracles take place. It was unexplainable.

It is not easy for people from that generation to explain how things happened in those early days, but people saw the miracles and believed. They believed in Jesus as their Lord and began to call themselves Christians. It was one of the few signs of hope in the dark days of Mao Zedong when evil seemed to consume all of China.

The first House Church in Lixin met together in his home. It was more of a hospital for the sick than a gathering place for believers because sick people who had no other hope for treatment would travel from far away to be miraculously healed. They came because they had heard the rumors of other sick being healed. Enguan prayed for them and they were indeed healed. This led to even more people believing and even more people telling their friends, family, and acquaintances about the miracles.

These things were taking place and the church was

growing, but they didn't have anything more than mere songs to rely on for their faith. They cherished those songs and held close to the prayers in the name of Jesus that showed power to heal the sick and perform miracles, but there was no Bible to be found anywhere. No one had ever even seen a Bible or knew anyone else who had.

In the 1980s there was a couple that were both Christians and the husband was seriously ill and about to die. One day his wife decided to get baptized. She thought that if she got baptized Jesus would see her and bless the water surrounding her. She was baptized and immediately collected the water around her in a bottle. She brought it to her sick husband and asked him to drink it. Amazingly, he drank from the water and was healed. Without a Bible there was no possible way for the people in Lixin County to understand the meaning of the miracles, but God responded to their misguided acts of faith anyway.

After some time the people of Lixin were finally able to get their hands on a Bible. The problem then was that they were not able to understand it. They were so excited to have a Bible, but were not exactly sure what to do with it, so when sick people came to their House Church meeting, they would place the Bible on the bed and tell people to go into the room with the bed and place their forehead on the Bible. Again people who were sick and did this were healed from their sickness. God was gracious in their ignorance.

After the people of the Lixin Church received a Bible they employed two main methods to heal the sick. One way was to have the Bible on the bed and have the sick people lay on it. Sometimes they even used the Bible like a pillow and would just lay on it and believe in their healing.

The second way was to hit people with the Bible. The Lixin Church would get the sick people to stand still and they would take the Bible and actually hit them on the head. Amazingly, both ways worked.

In 1984, Dennis Balcombe gave Enguan his first Bible. "Bao Dani (Dennis) would often bring in groups, sometimes up to fifty people, who would bring in the Bible. It was not easy to get a Bible during those days. We didn't have mobile phones to contact people and a delivery of Bibles often involved a lot of waiting and misunderstandings. During one delivery of Bibles, Mr. Z—one of the delivery truck drivers—was arrested. The police took the entire truckload of Bibles into custody. On another occasion Mr. Z drove the Bibles to the location that he was given. He dropped off the Bibles and returned home. The next day he called the leaders only to discover that he had dropped off the Bibles at the wrong location."

In the 1980s and even into the 1990s the believers went from home to home and county to county spreading the Good News of Jesus Christ. Enguan was given a bicycle and would ride it from six in the evening until noon the next day just to minister in different areas.

The Lixin Network became notorious among the local police in Anhui during those days because most of the Christians arrested during that time were from the Lixin Network. Enguan recalls,

> We were one of the most heavily-persecuted churches in all of China. The police regularly swept through our area and conducted sting operations. Every year more than one hundred leaders would be arrested. Christians in our area were not Christians for long before they were rounded up by the police. You would have one believer who had been a believer for six years and had served five and a half of those years in prison. It was not uncommon to have believers that were baby Christians only being saved for a month or more before being martyred for their faith. This was life in the Lixin Network. Those were hard days.

> In 1998, I remember that we had a large meeting with so many leaders who came from all over China. They were all referring to themselves as Lixin House Church workers, but many of them were not from Lixin County, so in 1998 when we were in that meeting we came together and made the decision to change our name from Lixin to Mongfu. It seemed to be more appropriate than Lixin.

> In 1998 we actually came together to focus on training up other leaders. All of us in the top leadership positions were positive that we would all soon end up in jail. We were concerned for the future of the church in Anhui if we all ended up in jail at the same time. The Public Security Bureau was searching for us and we knew that it was only a matter of time before we were caught. We could not run forever.

> All of us leaders came together and began to talk

about the bare essentials that a replacement should know in case anything ever happened to us. A young man at the meeting wrote down everything that we dictated to him. He wrote up a list of everything that would be needed in our absence. The young brother also wrote down all of the names of everyone at the meeting. Unfortunately, that brother posted it on the Internet and caused us all a lot of problems.

Because of intense persecution, Enguan still keeps a low profile. When those making the documentary *The Cross in China* came to China, he did not want to be interviewed by them. *The Cross in China* is a set of stories and interviews about the Chinese House Church that were put on DVD and sold around the world.

In the 1990s the Lixin Church began to arrange more formal training for its leaders. They would study the Bible and evangelism. Upon completing the training, the students were sent out to areas all over China. Anhui people tend to be good stage performers; so many students went to minority areas in China like Yunnan Province and arranged stage productions that would present the gospel in small villages. These young men and women used a traveling stage show to present the gospel and traveled from village to village.

So many people came to the Lord through that ministry, but it did have challenges. Due to China's one child policy there are not enough females around for the men to marry so on a couple of occasions the Lixin female evangelists were invited to villages to perform their play, only to be kidnapped and forced into marriages.

In 1999 Enguan was arrested and went to jail for two years. During that time he was forced to make boxes for Haier electronics. Today Haier is a famous brand in China and is even becoming popular worldwide. During his time in prison he shared a cell with about forty other prisoners.

"I was never really bothered by my time in prison, to be honest. I really felt that since all of my coworkers had already gone to prison or were still in prison it was my turn now."

During his time in prison, he remembers clearly that there was one brother in prison with him. He was only in for about eight months and had been put on death row. He knew that he was about to be executed and instead of living every day in fear, he put his trust in the Lord and preached the gospel to everyone else on death row. Even though they were in the most hopeless situation with no light at the end of the tunnel, they found love and mercy in Christ. Everyone on death row in that prison became a Christian.

Enguan knows Pastor Zhang Rongliang from Fangcheng Church because Pastor Dennis Balcombe had introduced them. There were some major problems between the Fangcheng and Lixin Networks, but the two leaders met, talked through their problems, and prayed about the challenges together.

Those challenges usually arose when evangelists from the two networks would arrive in the same place to preach the gospel and end up in competition, but a solution was eventually worked out. Today the two brothers are highly respectful of one another.

In the past ten years there have been some major shifts in the way that Blessing Church conducts their operations in China and abroad. The people are better prepared and are given many more tools to use on the field than in the past. Today, one of the closest visions to their heart is the Back to Jerusalem vision. The young people in Lixin Church are really passionate about taking the gospel to the darkest regions of the earth and to see those who have never heard the gospel of Jesus Christ saved.

Their evangelists have been heading out in large numbers to share the gospel in areas like Tibet, Guangxi, Guizhou, and Yunnan. Some of them are working at the universities and preaching the gospel to the students. In the beginning, many of these workers were able to get support from Teacher Zhao and Brother Ren, but in 2008 and 2009 the support decreased because of the drop in financial support from the West.

This affected the number of workers Lixin was able to send to the western regions of China, but those workers survived on faith. Today they are encouraging the local churches to support the workers with what they have. Some of the areas in south western China have been doing well for ten years and they really thank Teacher Zhao for his hard work and dedication in ensuring that they had extra support to cultivate those areas at the beginning.

Many of the churches that were planted ten years ago have grown and flourished remarkably. Guangxi has been one of the areas of heaviest focus for Lixin. It has not been an easy road because the evangelists from Anhui are Han Chinese and don't speak the minority languages of the mountain villages in Guangxi.

Evangelists from Lixin Church have had to overcome numerous cultural and linguistic barriers to do ministry there.

Today Lixin has Bible training centers all over China. They are also starting to get involved in humanitarian projects in poor areas that can be used as avenues for preaching the gospel. In 2011 they began to work on helping people in a small rural village obtain clean water. Previously the villagers had to walk about ten kilometers to get potable water.

Enguan looks back at the past and compares it with the present in China. "Things are changing in China. Before there were so many police after me who wanted to arrest me and throw me into prison. Today I am a bit older and so are they. Instead of chasing me, we might even go out and have a cup of tea together. Of course if we have a meeting they will not be happy about it and will come and break it up. They are obligated to take down the names of everyone present, but for the most part we have come to terms with each other."

Enguan had just received his first passport. He has been able to travel to Hong Kong and for the first time in March, 2011 he was able to travel to America. "I didn't have anything to do there," he chuckled. "I just wanted to go and see what it was like."

Before we parted after the interview that night, there was one message he asked me to share with the West on behalf of the Lixin House Church Network. The message was that there is still a desperate need for Bibles in China. "Please share with your partners in America and Europe that believers in China still need Bibles. This is one of our daily challenges and we cannot do it alone."

16

LITTLE JOE'S NETWORK

Little Joe's network is named after its founder, although Joe is obviously not his real name nor is it the name of his network, but to use real names would jeopardize the network because it has never been written about. Little Joe works with very few foreigners. In fact we don't believe he works with any foreigners outside of those partnered with Back to Jerusalem.

This network is considered to be a fragment of the Blessing Network that has gone rogue, although Little Joe's father had always been a quite independent pastor within that network. When Little Joe's father was in prison in the 90s, Little Joe began to be recognized as the one taking the reins of the underground House Church network.

His name comes from the Chinese way of saying "Junior." In western terms, his father would be "Joe Senior," but Chinese say *xiao*, meaning "little," to denote sons who share names with their fathers. Little Joe is relatively young for a network pastor, having been born in Fengyang County, Anhui Province in May of 1973. Among all the House Church leaders in China he is one of the most dependable when it comes to financial reporting and project clarity. The author has traveled extensively with Little Joe for several years and often shares a hotel room with him, and thus has spent much time sharing stories and discussing future plans and visions with the pastor.

Little Joe first visited the United States in 2011 soon after receiving his first passport. It is not easy for House Church pastors to obtain a passport since most of them have criminal records, but somehow Little Joe was approved to receive this valuable travel document. That trip to the US was only his second time outside of China. Having already been to a foreign country once before improved his chances of getting a US visa, so our organization had arranged his first trip abroad as well.

Little Joe's network is one of the smaller networks in China and is estimated to be from eight hundred thousand to one million believers. This network is mainly established in a rural part of China, with most members being in Anhui Province.

Little Joe first started preaching in the 1990s and is the son of a preacher. He had always wanted to be a preacher like his father. At the outset of his ministry, the only support he received came from his parents who were extremely poor. Naturally, a father who is habitually being arrested is not the most ideal source of ministry funding. Little Joe remembers the early days when he felt the Lord calling him to preach the gospel in different areas far from home.

The beginning of Little Joe's network was similar to that of other Chinese networks, marked by miracles and many sick being healed.[24] In the early days they set out to start a church in a rural part of Anhui that was known for having many sick people. The farmers outside of that village had to walk a long way to attend the meetings and it was a very hot summer. There was one woman in particular who had heart problems and actually had a heart attack brought on by the strain of walking so far in the hot sun. Little Joe and his coworkers prayed for her and she was immediately healed. She said that she had had several heart attacks in the past and had needed to be taken to the hospital to get an injection in order to be revived, but this time she was immediately and completely healed.

A quite different story came from another village in Jiangsu Province. There was a sister there who had stomach cancer. She believed God would heal her cancer when she got saved, but her condition actually got worse after her salvation. When the doctor said she only had a few days to live, she was greatly discouraged and wanted to give up the faith. Little Joe and some elders came to the hospital to pray for her. She had been an idol worshiper in the past and it was clear that the demons didn't want to let go of her. While they were praying, the nurses came in and started yelling at them, saying, "What are you doing? Why are you starting a fire in here? You could burn the whole building down!" Evidently the presence of God was so strong in that room during their prayer that the nurses saw fire coming through the closed door. The darkness lifted and the woman repented, saying, "Lord, even though you didn't heal me, I will believe in You whether I die or not." She went to be with her Lord that same week.

Along with those kinds of miracles, there was also supernatural provision in those days. Little Joe felt the calling to go preach the gospel in other villages, but didn't have any money. He needed bus fare to travel to other churches that were in desperate need of preaching. There were occasions when he was able to visit churches in other villages, but didn't have the funds for a bus ticket home. One time he had to stay in a village and preach there for almost a month, not by choice, but because he didn't have any money to leave. He had other churches that needed him to come and preach, but he had no way of making his way to their village.

He loves to recall the story of how one Sunday he preached at a service in one village and only had half the required bus fare to get to his next preaching engagement. He decided to ride the bus as far as his money would take him and walk the rest of the way to the meeting. Unbeknownst to him, there was a fellow believer on the same bus. When he attempted to purchase the ticket before boarding he was informed that his ticket had already been paid for in full by the sister who just happened to be on the bus.

After preaching in the next church, he prayed, "God, you fed Elijah. Please provide a way for me to go home." Soon after he prayed a Christian sister arrived on a long distance bus from far away. She walked alone in the dark to where Little Joe was staying because she was determined to meet him. She told him, "God led me to see you now." After talking for a while she said, "God told me you don't have any transportation money," and insisted on giving him twice what he needed for the trip home.

This testimony may seem insignificant in comparison to others that have been told in China, but it was through this small provision that Little Joe learned at an early age to trust in the Lord. Through this experience he got a deep impression that God really does provide.

Little Joe's lowest point came in 2000 when he was arrested in Anhui Province. The police confiscated his phone, so he was deeply distraught that they would go through his address book and find all the phone numbers of his coworkers. This bothered him so much that he wasn't in the least concerned with his own safety or what would happen to him. He felt personally responsible for bringing disaster on his beloved coworkers, but he later found out that the police never looked up the numbers and no one else was arrested.

The judge sentenced Little Joe to three years in prison for preaching. It was arranged for him to be sent to an infamous coal mine labor camp to serve out his sentence. This was the same dreaded labor camp that his father had served in years before.

"The prison that my father went to was especially hard on Christians," Little Joe recalled.

I know that many Christians like to tell the stories that end in wonderful testimonies about God's amazing grace and power bringing them through the most trying times, but that was not always the case.

The coal mine was torture for Christians serving time there. Coal mining is one of the most dangerous and physically demanding jobs in China. [The Chinese government] likes to use Christians and political dissidents for labor in the coal mines. Many go in, but few come out. There was a brother who was in love with the Lord and was arrested in Anhui then sent to the labor camp. He was told to deny the name of the Lord. He refused. He was sent to the coal mine. He was again told to deny the name of the Lord. He again refused.

The guards beat him for refusing to deny the Lord. Every day every prisoner has a quota to complete. If they do not complete their quota they will be punished. After the brother was beaten, he was not able to complete his quota the next day. He was beaten again and kicked in the head. He was kicked so hard that it caused him serious damage.

He was not able to handle it any longer. He used a light in the shower room, took the light bulb out of the socket and then turned on the water and killed himself. He just couldn't take it anymore.

Torture for a few days or even weeks might be bearable, but when there is no end in sight, there can be times when the human body and mind just quit.

Little Joe had a friend in politics who was able to get his sentence reduced to one year and he was never sent to the coal mine. While he was in prison the prison guards would interrogate him night and day. "They would suddenly take me from my cell and interrogate me at the most unexpected times. They especially liked the middle of the night!" They chose the odd hours of the night and early morning to catch him off guard. The guards hoped to get him to incriminate himself, but with God's help he was able to endure the questioning. "I truly learned the truth of Luke 12:12, 'For the Holy Spirit will teach you in that very hour what you ought to say.'"

Little Joe's underground House Church network has one unique asset that deserves special recognition. They have a clear understanding of "Business as Mission." In 2011, Little Joe was one of the main speakers at a Back to Jerusalem Business as Mission Conference held in America's "Bible Belt."

Business as Mission (BAM) is a relatively new term, but is based on biblical concepts. Other expressions often used among missions strategists include 'transformational business,' 'tent-making,' 'great commission companies,' and 'kingdom business.'

BAM is part of a threefold interaction between churches, missionaries, and the Christian business community. This method of missions can cause quite the scene depending on the personalities, nationalities, and egos involved, but the intention of our organization (Back to Jerusalem) is to keep the parameters open when defining, teaching, and using it on the mission field. Definitions based on rigid western models often limit the effectiveness in practice because flexibility is key in both international business and missionary service.

Little Joe's network has been using business to support many of their ministers and ministries in China. Many people propound that the BAM concept is holistic in nature—believing that God wants to transform people and communities spiritually, economically, socially, and environmentally—but for the most part BAM is a means to an end with groups like Little Joe's. It can most definitely impact a community and possibly on occasion improve a local economy, but those factors don't affect BAM in our understanding of the term.

We often hear the phrase, "Let's keep business, business," meaning, "Let's keep business and missions separate." Even in some missionary circles people will say that business and missions shouldn't be mixed. We believe this to be a fatal error for those that are mission focused, which Back to Jerusalem definitely is. The vision of sharing the gospel drives everything that we do—including business.

The dichotomy between sacred and secular is not exactly biblical, but has deeply affected our views on work, business, church and missions. In America, it is derived from the concept of separation of Church and State. Today, the term has come to reflect the idea that religion and faith need to be quarantined from other aspects of secular life. However, life isn't made up of compartmentalized boxes, but is rather a ball of interconnected wires.

BAM is part of a wider global movement in the Chinese House Church and can be seen strongly in Little Joe's House Church network. The underground church in China is recognizing and responding to God's call to take the Good News of Jesus Christ to the whole world, *especially* to those areas that don't want it. Back to Jerusalem is not the first group to use the concept of Business as Mission. In fact, it is likely that many groups will be upset because they will feel that we are polluting the purity of the BAM concept. But the Chinese applications of BAM are unique in many ways from the western concept and will vary from country to country, business to business, and network to network.

A BAM business is typically defined from a western perspective as being a: (1) real, viable, sustainable and profitable business; (2) with a Kingdom of God purpose, perspective and impact; (3) leading to transformation of people and societies spiritually, economically, socially and environmentally; (4) to the greater glory of God. This definition is taken directly from another BAM training being taught around the world. These businesses are basically run by businessmen who have a desire to use their position and influence for the Kingdom of God. They are usually driven by opportunity, business viability, and the idea of using that opportunity to share the gospel with others, make a positive impact, and see people come to Christ.

At the 2010 Lausanne Conference in Cape Town, South Africa, a sixty-page report about Business as Mission was issued, called the *Business as Mission Manifesto (revisited from 2004/Document 142180)*. In short, it said that Business as Mission was about demonstrating God's love and Kingdom in a Christ-like manner by using business to meet the needs of the people, ultimately *ad maiorem Dei gloriam*—for the greater glory of God.

The troubling part of the document stated, "Unfortunately there is sometimes a confusing misuse of the term BAM. Let's be clear: BAM is not 'Business for Mission', a fundraising activity facilitated by the profits generated by business. Neither is BAM 'Business as Platform' i.e. an attempt to obtain visas to do 'real ministry'. Rather, genuine BAM is the practice of business as a calling and ministry in its own right, a manifestation of the Kingdom of God." Lausanne followers would undoubtedly be up in arms over the Chinese House Church version of BAM.

From observing House Church networks like Little Joe's, it can be concluded that—at least for the Chinese—BAM is: (1) business leaders using their influence and position to share the gospel; (2) church mission directors using business to fund their ministries; (3) missionaries using business as a platform for ministry.

Little Joe and his team of under-educated missionary misfits maintain a minority concept in mainstream western thought, but are taking advantage of the mainstream trends in countries in the 10/40 Window where mixing business, religion, and family is a common practice.

Respected academic institutions like Wheaton College and Biola University in USA have embraced BAM as it is defined by the Lausanne Conference. YWAM (Youth With A Mission) provides a highly professional six-week BAM training course where the idea of platforms and project funding is not only not embraced but outright rejected from their concept of BAM.

However, YWAM has also rightly admitted that BAM as it is taught and defined by the western world doesn't do so well in the 10/40 Window: "One of the biggest hurdles for BAM businesses around the world, especially in and around the so-called '10/40 Window,' is securing investment capital. BAM is not built on traditional models of charitable fundraising and donations, but on a foundation of the disciplined allocation and return of capital. One of the biggest challenges for the global BAM movement is the lack of BAM investment funds—capital managed with vision, professionalism, excellence and integrity." Basically, since the western concept of BAM doesn't allow for the businesses to be funded by ministries or vice versa, BAM projects in the 10/40 Window have a very hard time getting off the ground.

What is the definition for Business as Mission as practiced in China with Back to Jerusalem and underground House Church networks like Little Joe's? Well, defining anything Chinese isn't easy, because it involves absolutes and commitment to terms with defined parameters, concepts quite foreign to

Chinese business. The following definition may be the best "working" definition that can be given at this point: *BAM is any opportunity to use business to further the gospel of Jesus Christ.*

The definition had to be changed to be more inclusive. Other terms can be coined to describe each stage of the Chinese view of BAM, as many westerners might prefer, but basically their model is: (1) Business as Mission; (2) Business for Mission Support; (3) Business as Platform.

Even these three terms need to be used flexibly because they are often in harmony with each other in different stages of an outreach. For instance, in Egypt a Chinese businessman saw an opportunity to start a grocery store. He was a Christian, but his investment was mainly financial, not necessarily spiritual. He began to have problems with the business and found himself in jail. He soon after met Brother Yun, who helped bring focus and purpose to his life by reintroducing him to the Father who ordains our steps. The businessman then decided to use his business as a platform to give visas (and jobs) to Chinese missionaries. The Chinese who left China to work for him did not care if they were going to work in a grocery store or clean toilets at the local zoo—they were just looking for any opportunity to go to Egypt because they felt a strong calling to share the gospel with Muslims there.

The Back to Jerusalem missionaries working for the grocer work hard to earn their pay and are not reliant on other sources for feeding themselves, thus making this a Business for Mission. This kind of metamorphosis is common and happens often with the Chinese. It isn't uncommon to see all three facets occurring at the same time.

This Chinese understanding of BAM is not a definition cooked up by those doing years of research, study, and analysis of mission trends, but is part of a new trend that is becoming more and more common as the number of Christians in China increases.

As we saw, one of the problems admitted by the Cape Town Conference was the lack of Christian businesses to invest in BAM projects in the 10/40 Window. This goes without saying because legitimate businesses that focus on financial returns have to evaluate the risk and capital involved. Most of the countries in the 10/40 Window are volatile and have no real stability for a thriving business, making long-term predictions impossible. In that area, most business plans last less than a week after registration because everything is always changing.

Little Joe's network is part of a new trend among businesses in China where truly legitimate businesses are willing to donate to missionary projects that are in turn using business on the mission field. Such businesses aren't necessarily expecting a return on their investment, but are most interested in taking advantage of viable mission opportunities.

It is this concept of BAM that Little Joe brings to the western world as he travels with Back to Jerusalem representatives. He often shares about the BAM structure in China and uses examples of businesses in Shanghai that are intricate parts of his ministry vision.

17

OTHER NETWORKS & PERSONALITIES

There are several underground House Church networks in China that are often overlooked because they are not as large as the more well-known ones in Henan or Anhui Province. However, their work is having an impact in China and around the world.

These networks are playing an important role domestically as well as internationally. Some of these individual groups within the underground House Church deserve special recognition for their huge impact on the growth of the church in China.

"YL" Network

Today in China there are many younger leaders who operate in a similar fashion to pastor YL, who has rolled up his sleeves and is tackling the huge challenge of evangelizing in Shenzhen. YL is one of the leaders who were under the tutelage of Peter Xu. Though he still considers himself to be a disciple of Peter Xu, he has an independent vision and focus for Shenzhen.

Back to Jerusalem International has supplied Bibles to his network throughout China for many years. He has planted churches among minority groups in places like Guizhou, Guangxi, Yunnan, and Sichuan. Although he planted those churches more than ten years ago, he still visits them on a regular basis to continue the cultivation of those ministries. He sends many of his workers out of Shenzhen to witness and plant churches in the minority villages. He also had the vision to start the very first Christian House Church-run magazine in China.

When the earthquake hit Sichuan in 2008, YL's group was one of the first groups to respondMinistry workers from the church traveled into the areas that were hit the hardest and worked together with the locals to help them rebuild. They provided counseling and assistance. They wrote many of the testimonies and stories from the earthquake's aftermath in their new magazine and distributed the magazine throughout the country. The publication helped to build understanding between Christians and the unbelieving Chinese public at large. It also helped in the grieving process of many of the earthquake victims who were able to read the amazing stories of some of the survivors and how they found Christ in the darkest hour of their lives.

YL is currently living in Shenzhen and his network is heavily focused on the many workers who have flooded southern China to work in offices there. Today YL has several hundred thousand people in his network throughout China, but in Shenzhen specifically he is seeing more than fifty people per month come to the Lord.

"South China" Church

Like YL, South China Church is from Peter Xu's network. Gong Shengliang was considered to be one of its top leaders and was sentenced to death, but his sentence was later commuted to life imprisonment. South China Church continues to grow even though many of its leaders are in prison. Although it's impossible to know for sure, some have estimated the South China church to have over fifty thousand members.

At the same time, alleged and even confirmed wrongdoings by Gong Shengliang have limited the impact of this church. These would include allegations that he had inappropriate relationships with some female followers and had authorized imposing unorthodox methods on those who were not deemed loyal to his church.

To this day Pastor Gong is often beaten in prison and his face is scarred as a result. During family visits, other inmates have had to carry him from one place to another because he was too weak to walk. It has been reported that he was beaten so badly in 2003 that he nearly died.

Leaders like Xu Fuming and Sun Minghua are in prison as well. Sun Minghua's mother was a believer and played a major role in her salvation when she was almost twenty years old. She almost immediately began to serve the Lord and share the gospel with others. Minghua was arrested in September of 2001 for organizing a spiritual cult and influencing direct disobedience to the laws of China. She was sentenced to life in prison, but the sentence was later reduced to twelve years. Other members of her network also suffered. During that same year, more than five hundred South China full-time evangelists were detained and beaten, had their homes raided, and had property confiscated.

During this particular crackdown in September, the government had pulled out all the stops in persecuting the South China Church. They planned to secretly execute several leaders without a real trial. At that time members of the church contacted us asking if we could help save the lives of their leaders. We began to send out prayer requests by email, but clearly more was required. We began looking for a lawyer to help with the case.

We engaged a lawyer to help fight for the lives of the South China Church's leaders, but it was to no avail. Chinese lawyers were not able to make any leeway without the aid of international pressure. By God's grace that came from an unlikely source: United States President George W. Bush.

Unfortunately for those who wanted to swiftly and quietly snuff out the leadership of the South China Church, President George Bush was scheduled to visit China the next month. We asked the family members of the imprisoned leadership to write letters about the situation and then asked one of our influential Southern Baptist friends for the American Ambassador's personal phone number. We made the call and the following conversation ensued:

"Hello?"

"Hello, I have some very important letters that I need to send to you via fax. We have friends who are in prison and will be executed in China for their Christian faith. We need to get a message to the President. Do you have a secure fax line?"

There was silence on the other line. Everything had been laid out on the table from the start.

"I am sorry, who is this?"

"I am a friend of a friend."

It was beginning to sound like something from an old spy film, but the Ambassador amazingly replied,

"OK, here is the fax number...."

Once we had the number we faxed the family members' letters to the American Embassy in Beijing. We later learned that the messages did get through to President Bush and that diplomatic channels were employed on behalf of the leadership. There were immediate results. We were able to hire a team of lawyers to fight on behalf of the seventeen members of the South China Church leadership and--after much pressure and a new court case--none of them were executed. We unfortunately later found out that some of the Chinese government's accusations against Pastor Gong were indeed true, so he wasn't released.

Ten years later, on Christmas Day 2011, Li Ying--a Christian newspaper editor and niece of Pastor Gong—was released from prison as one of those seventeen members whom God rescued from execution. They may never know how many brothers and sisters in Christ were praying for them and acting on their behalf during that crucial time.

Benjamin

Just a few miles north of YL's headquarters is a small group in Guangzhou that was started by a young man who never knew his father. His wife was born and raised in Taiwan and both of them are rather famous singers today. Benjamin (his English name) is not a network leader, but leads several groups in China and has greatly influenced the house churches with his music. Benjamin started a small Bible study group in his home in Guangzhou in the late 1990s.

In early 2000, Guangzhou was a booming city experiencing exponential growth every year and many young educated Chinese were coming to the Lord in the wealthier suburban areas. Suburban areas were a new concept in China at the time. A television sitcom was released in China around this time that captured this new culture called, "Jia You Er Nu." It is about a Chinese suburban family that has one son and one daughter and lives in a moderately wealthy area.

Benjamin pushed the limits of what China was ready to accept as a society when in 2003 he went on national television to compete in a singing competition much like "American Idol." He and his wife sang a Christian song with his two children, one boy and one girl, in front of several million people. The audience was blown away when they heard the family sing about loving one another.

Benjamin won the competition and moved to Beijing where he began working on a recording contract. There he met with the well-known actor and movie producer Shaun Bao.

Shaun Bao

Bao is not a traditional House Church leader, but he is having a huge impact on the church in China. He is an iconic leader that has made headlines around the world.

"They call me the last actor of China," Shaun said in a 2006 interview at his home in Beijing. It was a tongue-in-cheek reference to the movie, *The Last Emperor*. Shaun is very energetic and his enthusiasm is contagious. He is continuously pushing the boundaries in China.

He oversees several house churches throughout Beijing and has built a massive facility for training tomorrow's Chinese Christian leaders. In 2007, he legally published in China a biography of Jesus, which was overtly evangelistic in nature. Today he teaches business concepts for Christians in China.

Shaun was born into the royal family of China—a three-hundred-year-old dynasty that quickly found itself being persecuted in Mao's new China after 1949. His family, like any educated or wealthy family in China during the rise of Communism, was considered to be a part of the "black class." This class was made up of professionals like doctors, professors, and business owners. All their wealth was stripped from them and they were forced into re-education camps and farm labor.

Shuan's mother and father were forced to go to different areas to serve in the field for the "betterment" of China's masses. However, in his youth, Shaun caught the eye of Mao's wife who thought that he should be a film star. As a result, Shaun starred in the very first movie to be shown in China after the Communist revolution. Shaun later starred in twelve additional films over a period of just eight years.

As one of the few Chinese privileged enough to go abroad at the time, he left China at the age of twenty-five and moved to New Zealand. With no money or resources of any kind, he took jobs cleaning floors, doing laundry, and babysitting to support himself.

He had no future in New Zealand. He was living off of minimum-wage jobs in a country that was not his home. He lacked family or friends to support him financially or emotionally, but returning to China would have been even more of an embarrassment and would have marked him as a complete failure. Shaun had hit rock bottom with no hope in site, but then he was attacked by a German shepherd. How desperate his situation must have been if he considered being attacked by a rabid dog as one of the highlights of that time.

After the attack he was approached by a believer who spoke Mandarin and introduced him to Christ. Shaun had never heard of Jesus Christ before. The only god-like personality he had ever heard about was Mao Zedong. After meeting with Christians, he was amazed at the love and care they had for him. He felt accepted and loved. He gave his life to Christ and immediately became focused on his homeland. Shame was no longer an overwhelming factor. Returning to China to share about the Jesus he had never heard about until he moved to New Zealand became a primary focus.

Shaun saw the need for Bibles in China and began to help get Bibles into the country while leading several mission groups to Beijing. He eventually moved back to China and began preaching the gospel. He started a home group that began to grow beyond capacity. He then sent representatives out to start other churches throughout the city.

Today, there are more than fifty churches throughout China that are directly connected with Shaun and even more in his vast network of connections. These churches are in more wealthy areas, so the Christians have been active in sending and supporting missionaries abroad.

Shaun Bao and Zhao Ming are among the more youthful urban leaders in China who are leading the charge to see China officially embrace Christianity. Unlike most House Church believers in China, they see themselves as Christian ambassadors and try to make everything open and legitimate. They are fighting the good fight and are slowly gaining ground.

Benjamin and Shaun Bao are now making movies and music that reach out to China's new generation and are appealing to a wide audience among the urbanites. They are creating high-quality entertainment with a strong gospel message and the response is amazing. These mediums are surely changing China one person at a time.

Xiao Min

Benjamin and his Bible group in Guangzhou worked together to make one of the first Christian music videos ever produced in China for the underground House Church. He took the music of Xiao Min—one of the most famous underground Christian music writers in all of China—and performed them in different settings to distribute to the underground churches.

We worked together in those early years to print and distribute tens of thousands of those music VCDs (Video Compact Discs) throughout China. Unlike in the western world where a Christian can go to any Christian bookstore or shop online for Christian materials, things are much more complicated in China. This was really the first time such a project had ever been done. The VCD was called the "Canaan Songs."

Though Xiao Min is not a network leader, her songs have strengthened millions of believers in China's House Church. The Canaan Songs are the most popular among underground house churches in China today.

Those who want to get a taste of the suffering and pain that the Chinese church has gone through need only to listen to the messages in these songs. The Canaan Songs were written by a young girl who was born to poor peasant farmers in Fangcheng. It is only by God's grace that Xiao Min has been so influential. She is not educated or outgoing, but very shy and doesn't seem to know the first thing about music. She doesn't play an instrument or have a flashy stage presence, nor does she sit around with other great recording artists and discuss the ins and outs of the music business. Here is someone so meek that her singing cannot be heard unless the entire room is silent. She is just a simple farm girl that God used to write more than one thousand hymns that have been sung by persecuted believers all over China.

When Xiao Min was born she was unwanted by her parents. They wanted to give her away after her birth, but a big flood hit their village and prevented them from following through with their plan. Xiao Min dropped out of school when she was young and started to work in the cotton fields to help support her family. It was there that she heard the gospel for the first time. She was invited to her first church meeting while working in the field with a friend and at that meeting she gave her heart to Christ. She became a Christian completely against the wishes of her family. She secretly attended the church meetings without telling her parents.

In 1990, she felt the power of the Holy Spirit during one of those secret underground meetings and it was after that meeting that she wrote her first hymn. She later sang the hymn to a little girl in her village and the little girl went around singing the song. When others asked the little girl where she had heard the song, she replied that she had learned it from Xiao Min.

The songs began to spread like wildfire. They were unique to Chinese life, unlike the hymns that had been taught by foreign missionaries many years earlier. Xiao Min wrote hymns that expressed exactly what the Chinese church was going through and they ministered to the leaders who were being persecuted at that time.

Xiao Min is a prime example of the unique qualities of the Chinese House Church. She has neither education nor wealth. Despite all those worldly shortcomings—or rather because of them—God used her to move His people in China.

After seeing how her songs were reaching people in China and helping them through hard times, Xiao Min began to pray to go to prison. She actually prayed that God would send her to jail for the sake of the gospel so that she could identify better with those who were suffering for Christ's name. Her prayer was answered. Two years after she had become a Christian, the police raided a meeting she was at. On December 7, 1992 the police burst through the doors and apprehended everyone at the prayer meeting. The quiet and shy farm girl became the object of intense interrogation. She was slapped around and beaten, but insists that she was not treated as badly as the others.

> After being arrested, she wasn't scared at all.
>
> Furthermore, she said that on one summer day when it was extremely hot she requested the guard to let everyone wash their head, but she received a rude response telling her to ask the Lord Jesus to wash for them.
>
> Despite the rude response, the Canaan Hymn author was not discouraged, but she used this as an inspiration to write the number 56 hymn "Lord, We Know Deeply" in the Canaan Hymns series.
>
> In this hymn, Xiao Min wrote, "Lord we know

deeply that in every moment your love never, never diminishes, Lord we know deeply that in every moment, our only friend is you, our hearts long for you, our hearts long for you, because you're the first in millions, no one can be compared with you, no one can be compared with you."[25]

During her time in prison, her parents began to blame her for their problems. A message was sent to Xiao Min from her father stating that he was losing weight worrying about her and that the family really needed her help on the farm to survive. She was told by her family to abandon her silly beliefs, deny Christ and get out of jail. Xiao Min lovingly refused. She clung to the name of Jesus and refused to let go of her faith in Him. Her family abandoned her and her country was punishing her.

Her release would have been as easy as saying, "I don't believe in Jesus anymore." All of her problems would seemingly have gone away if she had just denied Christ, but instead of fleeing from her problems, she provided comfort to her fellow inmates and began to sing in the midst of it all. When the other prisoners heard this, they too began to rejoice.

Today Xiao Min continues to write songs that speak directly to the underground House Church in China and is greatly influencing the direction of tomorrow's Chinese church. She has the desire to go and preach the gospel in Africa and the Middle East as well.

Benjamin, Shaun Bao, and Xiao Min are able to work with all of the House Church networks or none of them at all. They have the unique position in China to go between networks to build bridges as well as pave the way for more religious freedom in China for tomorrow. This dynamic trio is making an especially huge impact in the capital city of Beijing. There are churches today in Beijing that started out as simple independent home groups and have grown into more formal church gatherings. They are not registered, but are not hiding their identities either. They are also not intentionally provoking problems. They intentionally don't do things that they know will highlight their illegal activities and the police purposefully ignore them. It is a mutual understanding of convenience.

The police do not want a bad name with the people and

the people don't want problems from the police. They do, however, want to be free to worship Christ and they would like to introduce others to Him as well. Groups like these continue to push the boundaries.

Today in Beijing there are many bookstores that are actually illegal Christian bookstores. They are legally registered and are selling Christian books legally printed in China, so they are left alone for the most part. They are recognized as bookstores and allowed to continue their operations with very little, if any, problems.

When the first few Christian bookstores opened around 2003 to 2005, there were raids and arrests, but after the dust settled, others also began to come in and find a way to work around the system. After some time, the effort just became tiring and the police had more important problems to deal with so they were left alone.

A Shandong Network

Things are much different in Shandong Province, where remnants of the early twentieth century movements are still strong. We cannot mention the names or the cities this network works in because that would indict their leadership. There are Christian gatherings in those cities that are open secrets and to mention places or names would jeopardize the operations there. This network in Shandong is pushing forward a strong movement that is also going against the local authorities.

Unlike Beijing, the area of this network's activity is not a large, progressive metropolis. In fact it more resembles Fangcheng in Henan Province or Lixin in Anhui Province. The leader, Mr. C, is an older leader who remembers the revivals in China from years ago and can still sing the songs of those early church meetings.

Mr. C is well known among the brothers in Henan Province. When Brother Yun and his wife were on the run from the police and forced into hiding, Mr. C and his wife took care of Isaac and Yiling, Yun's two children.

His activities and network have never been formally written about, but he has built up an extensive network whose numbers are not quite clear. From the rural farm areas of Shandong to the tourist cities like Qingdao they have created a massive movement that has connections with people in many different walks of life.

Mr. C is a businessman as well as a House Church pastor. He doesn't look for support from his church because his business takes care of all ministry needs. Mr. C uses the profits from the business to further the Kingdom work.

Their church does outreach to the rural schools by taking Christmas gifts to the children who live in the small villages. When the gifts are delivered the House Church representatives are then able to openly preach the message of Jesus Christ—in Communist public schools. They are able to do this because they know believers who are teachers and principals at several different schools. This network continues to grow among the business and farming communities. They have just started a training school that holds classes at the meeting place they recently finished building.

This church in Shandong is training up missionaries to be sent abroad as well. The daughter of Mr. C has been studying Korean and is preparing to preach the gospel to those on the Korean Peninsula.

Nanyang Network

Aside from Peter Xu, Tanghe, and Fangcheng, there is another independent movement in Nanyang that is one of the oldest networks still surviving in China. Very little is known about it because they have very little contact with foreigners.

Brother Yun is one of the more well-known leaders to emerge out of this group, but he was very connected with other leaders in China during his time as an active leader there. It isn't easy for a westerner to meet with people from this group because the leaders are still very entrenched in the rural areas and show up in muddy shoes and work clothes, causing them to stick out in any hotel.

Their leadership seems to be less centralized as well. This group is one of the most buried underground groups in all of China. According to Paul Hattaway, the Nanyang Church was founded by Elder Fu after he moved to Nanyang in the 1960s.[26]

Although we have financially supported this group's evangelists and provided them with cameras to film their current activities, their past history is not as well documented as the other networks. From what we been able to gather from field reports, the leadership is elderly and still strongly focused on rural evangelism. Although it is difficult to know for sure, today their evangelists appear to be working on farms and maintaining moderate church growth.

It is also difficult to get an idea of the size, number, and influence of this church. Brother Yun is one of their main representatives and still maintains a very close connection with the elders, but his living outside of China makes it difficult for him to acquire hard data from them. They are affectionate towards him and care about him deeply, which must not have been easy to maintain after his long absence from China.

Nanyang seems to be lost in time. The rest of China is changing all over, even in remote places like Tibet, but somehow Nanyang has been passed by and is still one of the most tightly-controlled hotspots in China today. This atmosphere is no doubt a contributor to the current security situation of the Nanyang Church.

What is for sure, however, is that the church in Nanyang continues to aggressively share the gospel with almost no foreign support or connections. They also have a deeply passionate connection to the Back to Jerusalem vision.

Enoch Wang

Enoch Wang remains a controversial figure in China to this day. Back to Jerusalem International has information about him mainly thanks to our relationship with his eldest daughter and her family. Susanne and her husband have been missionaries in Egypt for more than five years and are currently living and studying at a Bible school in California. We helped them get visas and a funding base in Egypt. Susanne actually gave birth to a son in Cairo.

Though Enoch Wang is controversial, the amount of suffering he has endured for the gospel is more than most people can imagine. One night in Cairo Susanne shared about the hard times her family went through in China for the sake of Christ. While sitting by the Nile River on a warm evening in Cairo, Susanne began to cry as she recounted what she had experienced in her early years.

Her father was a follower of Watchmen Nee's teachings. Watchmen Nee was a famous author and Christian leader in China who died in prison at the hands of the Communists. Enoch Wang was viewed as a traitor. He was a leader in public service to the People's Liberation Army and the Communist Party, but when it came out that he was a Christian leader, he was sent to prison for thirteen years.

"My mother and I felt abandoned," she said. "I was rejected from every school. We were yelled at and forced out on the street. We had nothing to eat or any way to get food. My mother and I were forced to beg. They were hard times for all of us."

After Enoch Wang was released from prison he tried to make things better with his family, but the immediate demands of the ministry drowned out his family's needs. After his release in 1994, he was arrested again in 1997 and spent another three years in prison, but not before tragedy struck their family.

Susanne was eighteen in 1997 and at home caring for her sister. She was holding her sister when she got too close to the balcony of their four story high apartment, lost her grip on the squirming child, and the infant fell four floors to a pile of bricks and stone rubble below. The baby's skull was cracked open and her brain was exposed. Blood was everywhere.

The baby died and the guilt that Susanne felt was more than could be explained. She had killed her sister. Because they were on the run from the police they couldn't even think about taking the baby to the hospital. All hope was lost.

However, after a day of prayer while Enoch was away at unity meeting with Sinim Fellowship members, her sister began to show signs of life. Air came back into her lungs and her heart began to beat again, putting color back in her face. On the third day, the baby began to walk again and eventually was completely healed. Today she shows no signs of having any brain damage. In response to her family's desperate prayers and hopeless situation, God had raised her back to life and completely healed her.

Enoch Wang struggled with family problems and today is estranged from Susanne and her mother, but he has kept on serving the Lord in China and focusing on the Back to Jerusalem vision.

Like all of the leadership in China, Enoch Wang is not perfect, but he is in love with Jesus Christ and has the track record to prove it. Much of his adult life has been spent in prison for preaching and today he continues to lead people to Christ. He also helps Chinese missionaries go to other countries. He now has a passport and is able to travel around the world to give counsel for helping Chinese missionaries get established in the countries between China and Jerusalem.

18

WENZHOU

Wenzhou is a powerhouse port city just south of Shanghai. Because of its good natural harbors and favorable location it is a natural center for trade. In the year 192, Wenzhou was the capital of the Kingdom of the Eastern Ou. During those days it was called the City of the White Deer. As folklore has it, when the city was being built a white deer passed by with a flower in its mouth.

Shortly after China's embarrassing defeat in the Second Opium War, several foreign-occupied cities were established on the mainland. Wenzhou was one of these foreign treaty ports, but unlike places like Shanghai, it was never really occupied by foreigners. The Chinese themselves ended up developing this port for trade.

Wenzhou was well-known for producing paper, silk, shoes, belts, and tea as well as shipbuilding in the past, but today is the largest producer of cigarette lighters, eyeglasses, and leather products.

Wenzhou is also well-known for having a huge number of Christians. It was one of the first places in China where the Communist government openly admitted defeat. The number of Christians in Wenzhou was just too high and after thirty years of persecution authorities came to the conclusion that the persistent faith couldn't be stamped out. At one point the Chinese government was reported by the *New York Times* as saying that ten percent of all Christians in China were in Wenzhou alone.[27]

Unregistered churches in Wenzhou built meeting places throughout the city with large red crosses prominently displayed on the steeples. The government attempted to destroy all these buildings in the 1990s and bulldozed many to the ground, but today they are back up again and are packed with believers.

The Chinese government's main excuse for giving up in the area is that there were already large numbers of Christians in

Wenzhou prior to the rise of Communism. Similar to the minority areas in Yunnan and Guangxi Provinces, where cultural traditions and religions are allowed to continue, Wenzhou Christianity was accepted as part of the culture. Today there are more than 1,200 registered churches in Wenzhou which enjoy a special situation in China. They are allowed to operate in quasi-registered mode yet maintain a high level of autonomy.

Pastor Phillip leads a registered church in Wenzhou. He has a church of about five thousand people in the heart of the city and is perfect for doing a case study on churches in Wenzhou. As a registered pastor in Wenzhou, he is supposed to be controllable. He is not allowed to travel to lead churches in other areas or run Sunday schools for children. However, Pastor Phillip is not being held back by the government in any of those areas.

This just shows the amount of autonomy given to the church in Wenzhou. It is not something brought up in the government-sponsored *China Daily* or paraded at annual meetings in Beijing, but this freedom is allowing churches in Wenzhou to have a huge impact on China and the world.

Even though some of the churches in Wenzhou are legal, many of them send out missionaries and evangelists—highly illegal activities.

In 2002, Pastor Phillip was in need of assistance in one of the poorer provinces in China and contacted Back to Jerusalem International for help. He had sent out a missionary who was working in rural areas and needed help establishing some orphanages. The author met with Pastor Phillip and his wife in a distant part of western China. Most of the underground House Church leaders in China do not have great relationships with their spouses, as they are often absent from home for months or even years at a time. It was nice to see that he had a great relationship with his wife and their ministry together was powerful as a result of their unity. They are also an amazing example to others.

After meeting at the train station we traveled together to meet with the local politicians to discuss the possibility of building orphanages. Having worked in China on similar projects for many years, we had assumed it was clear to everyone that ministry would have to remain clandestine.

We met with the local government officials and they drove us to a rural mountain area with very bad road conditions. Our first stop was a small roadside building in a rural town.

"We are here at the first church," the driver announced. We thought that maybe there was a misunderstanding, but Pastor Phillip confirmed that we were indeed at the first church a missionary from his church had planted in the area. The van left us there and everything seemed suspicious to the point that we were considering exit strategies for when the police returned. It was at that point that Pastor Phillip told the whole story.

> You see, one day at our church we had a young man who had come to Wenzhou to make money. After some time, he felt empty inside and felt a strong desire to come to our church and give his life to the Lord. After learning about the love and mercy of Jesus Christ he knew that he couldn't remain in Wenzhou and make money while his family back home was on their way to hell. He came to me and told me that he felt a calling to return home and preach the gospel to his family and the other surrounding villages. I told him that our church would support his efforts if he would go and share the gospel in this unreached area.
>
> A few months later he was arrested by the police for evangelizing, but then something strange happened. Instead of sending him to court to face a sentencing in prison, he was asked about his Christian beliefs. You see, the local police live in this poor area as well. They are not some foreign group sent here by the regime in Beijing. They are minorities with families at home who have to endure the same poverty as everyone else. They are looking for truth just like everyone else. The police had never met a Christian before, but they had heard that Christians help people who are poor, so they approached the evangelist that our Wenzhou Church sent here and asked him if he knew anyone who would be willing to help orphans. The evangelist called me from prison and I called you so we are now both here. This is one of the first churches that our Wenzhou church helped start.

Since this was such an unbelievable situation, our workers were very skeptical until an hour later when the government vehicle pick us up as promised and proceeded to take us to one church after another. None of these churches were registered and none of the believers were meeting in registered facilities. These were clearly unregistered churches with illegal activity, but no one seemed to care.

Over dinner that night, the local governor was clear about his need for help with the orphans and Pastor Phillip was clear about his need to share the gospel no matter what he did and no matter what subject we were talking about. If the governor talked about how nice the day was, the pastor would agree and say, "This is the day that the Lord has made. I will rejoice and be glad in it." If the officials would complement the pastor and his wife for how young they looked, he would reply by saying, "The joy of the Lord is my strength."

This banter-like dialog reached a climax when the foreign Back to Jerusalem representative exclaimed, "Mmmm, this Coke is good," and the pastor replied, "You know what else is good? God! God is good." Then with a full audience of every local government official in town—including the chief of police—he began to speak.

> Do you know what I find amazing? As you look around at China what do you see? I see poverty. I see lack of originality. I see poor people begging for scraps from western countries. To build an orphanage we have to depend on the kindness of strangers from western countries.
>
> What do you think makes these countries wealthy? What do you think makes these countries blessed? You know, I grew up in a Communist society just like everyone of you here did. I listened and believed everything that my teacher told me about God being a crutch for the weak and the opiate of the masses. I believed them when they told me that there is no God and believing in a fantasy will only make my situation worse.
>
> Look at Europe. Their history is rooted deeply in the belief that Jesus Christ is Lord. Does that make them weak? Does that make them poor? How are they doing compared to us?
>
> Look at America. They are a Christian nation. Does that make them weak? Does that make them intellectually inferior to us enlightened ones who think that God does not exist? Why are their academic institutions which

started off as missionary sending schools now some of the best in the world? Why are the schools and hospitals that missionaries started here still the very best in China?

Everything is better in America. Their educational facilities, their medical facilities, their working conditions, their programs for the poor, and even their leisure activities are some of the most sought after in the world.

Are Americans smarter than the Chinese? Many Americans come from Chinese descent so that cannot be the reason. The reason is because they believe in Jesus Christ.

Look at Korea. North Korea and South Korea are on the same peninsula. They have the same history with the same language and the very same culture. One end of the peninsula has freedom for Christians and has the world's largest church and the other enforces atheism. Which Korea is poor? Which Korea has dilapidated medical and educational facilities?

If we want to see China blessed, if we want to see our nation succeed, then we must accept Jesus Christ as our Lord and Savior. He is the Way and the Truth. There is nothing in this world truer than Him and the blessings He provides."

Every person in the restaurant stopped what they were doing for a brief moment while Pastor Phillip was talking. It was amazing. They were all nodding their heads in agreement with what he was saying.

We ended up not going through with the orphanage project, but supported a water sanitation project that brought clean water to a mountain village where the evangelist was working. After we completed that project, our representative traveled back to that area with Pastor Phillip and his evangelist. Almost the entire village had become Christian during the few months that it took to build the water sanitation plant and get running water into every home for the first time. The village leader hosted all of the church services in his home. All of them had abandoned their animistic beliefs and began following Christ.

Soon after the local governor got saved as well but was summarily fired when government higher-ups heard about his conversion. He was replaced with someone else who they thought would not be as susceptible to the teachings of the team from Wenzhou.

Since that first visit to the area with Pastor Phillip, the church in Wenzhou has sent several missionaries to the same minority area to conduct Christmas programs. They go from village to village performing Christmas plays. In some places they have even started churches where they perform the plays and lead people to Christ.

The church in Wenzhou has also played a pivotal role in changing the way that children are taught in Sunday schools. In the year 2000 an aforementioned meeting was held in Burma in which most of the main leaders of the underground House Church came together and talked about the needs of their churches in China. One of the main needs was a good Sunday school training program.

The leaders were very much aware of the need to reach out to the children in China. They came collectively to Brother Ren during the meeting in Burma and commissioned him to help meet this need in China. The job was passed to Sister Huang and the author. Sister Huang was in charge of the whole project. She is an unbelievable missionary who has been living and working in China for most of her life.

Her life is devoted to the people of China. She is a European missionary and her full Chinese name can be directly translated "the one who loves Chinese people." Sister Huang has never been married and doesn't have any children, but in China she has more children than she could ever physically give birth to. No book has ever been written about her and she isn't known by those outside of her ministry, but she has changed more lives than can be counted. A coworker testified of her,

> I began working with Sister Huang when I was helping the poor minority people in Yunnan Province and Tibet. We worked together to build schools and implement teaching programs and Sister Huang showed me how to serve the Chinese in the best way possible. She would walk up to one of the rural village schools and children with dirty faces would see us coming and become timid. She was not Chinese, so the children did not know how to react. She would just begin to show love and joy and in less

than five minutes the children would fall in love with her. Her joy is contagious and no one is ever able to resist it.

When Sister Huang was asked to take on the task of creating a program for Sunday school teachers in China, it was not a small task and she knew it. None of the Chinese House Church leaders had ever attended Sunday school. The Chinese only knew of life on the run. They only knew what it was like to survive as a church and had only had underground, illegal, clandestine church meetings for the last fifty years in China. Entire generations had come and gone without ever having been exposed to children's ministry. The only thing that the Chinese knew is that they didn't want their children's program to look like it did in the western world, which they considered to be a babysitting program while the parents were in the main service. The Chinese wanted a children's program that represented the real needs in China and on the mission field.

Sister Huang knew that she was not qualified, her experience was lacking, and her language was challenged. By God's wisdom, those all ended up being faculties of someone perfect for running the program. Experts on China never really make it far. They seem to usually know too much to allow them to be used by God and end up creating barriers that break the spirit of the people before they even start.

Sister Huang collected Sunday school training curriculum from around the world and presented it to the Chinese for review. Most mission organizations would have used their own judgment, selected materials, and forced it on the church. Instead, Huang painstakingly searched out training materials from around the globe and let the Chinese leadership decide. After several months they finally found one they liked.

The main husband and wife team in charge of using the materials was from New Zealand. The church in Wenzhou became the fertile ground for creation. Pastor Phillip and his church in Wenzhou took the project on as their main focus, investing everything needed for the program.

Sunday school teachers from different networks were carefully selected to travel to Wenzhou and train with the Kiwi trainers. The Sunday school teachers had one main focus: learn the material inside and out and then do what China is notorious for, copy it.

They would learn the material and master it in every way from a western perspective, then modify and bend it all around to make it fit a Chinese cultural setting. When they were finished it would look nothing like what it was in its original western format.

The training was intense. It went on for several weeks at a time over a period of more than a year. The teachers poured their hearts and souls into the training and gave the students everything they had. The students never wavered, but studiously took notes and eagerly drank every word being taught. Pastor Phillip and the Wenzhou Church had many business owners in their congregation who were able to provide perfect cover for the training sessions within their own facilities. At one point we were in a factory that made Oakley Sunglasses, whether they were genuine or cheap Chinese knockoffs is uncertain. We would sneak in early in the morning before the sun came up and quickly be ushered through the factory and up the stairs. There were workers above and below us busily making different types of sunglasses while we met.

The factory was owned by a Christian who attended Pastor Phillip's church in Wenzhou. He allowed us to use the facility as our training area and an entire floor was cleared out for us. We met, trained, and ate in that space.

One day we heard a noise downstairs and thought the police had come to arrest us. Pastor Phillip was called into the local police station for questioning. It ended up that the guards were just walking through and inspecting the work area when they saw someone breaking the security rules. Pastor Phillip knew the police well and they knew him. He never dealt with them as if they were enemies, but showed joy and love every time they were together.

Once the Chinese students had gleaned from the instructors from New Zealand all that they had to offer, they began to teach the material back to the instructors to ensure that they had learned it all correctly. Every session was filmed and immediately burned to a VCD that was in turn copied and handed out to the Chinese so they could take it back home and review each course over and over in their own language.

It was decided that the Chinese would use what they had learned to create an entire Sunday school training curriculum of their own that would be made into training module videos to be distributed throughout China. Sister Huang led the entire operation despite it being one of the most dangerous projects ever attempted in China. To this day sharing the gospel with anyone under the age of eighteen in China is illegal. The Chinese are very protective of the minds of children. They begin the Communist indoctrination process as early as three years old and continue the atheistic brainwashing for the rest of their lives. Any attempt to challenge this indoctrination by proselytizing a child is considered a grave offense and is dealt with swiftly and firmly in China.

The young leaders in Pastor Phillip's Wenzhou Church didn't flinch at the opportunity. They stood up and committed to a training that would eventually be one of the most widely-used Sunday school training programs ever.

Along with the training curriculum were sixteen hours of training module videos. All of the training, development, and filming were done in Wenzhou. The goal was to train Sunday school teacher-trainers who could go out and train other teachers. Each trainer allowed into the training would commit to train at least ten other teachers.

Pastor Phillip bravely did the introduction. We filmed him sitting at a small desk in a Wenzhou hotel room. He called it the "Dove Training Series." They developed a small black briefcase for each student to carry that contained the books for the students, training manuals for the teachers, as well as the sixteen training module VCDs. Many foreigners had different ideas for the name, but the church decided that Dove was the appropriate title. They created a small dove logo to go on the outside of the briefcase.

Pastor Phillip's church in Wenzhou was one of the first churches to begin using Dove and their children's church saw amazing growth. Children even began to invite other children to attend who would then go home and share the gospel with their parents.

This did not escape the notice of the local police department in Wenzhou. They threatened Pastor Phillip's church and forbade the church from teaching children about Jesus. This would not be allowed under any circumstances. However, Pastor Phillip surprisingly was willing to obey this rule under one condition.

"Every Sunday we have several thousand people come and worship at our church. Isn't that legal?" He asked the authorities. Knowing that his church was a legally-registered church in China, the police agreed.

"And every Sunday several thousand people come to our

church, so what do you want us to do with their children? According to you they cannot sit in the service with their parents so we have to create another activity for them. If you will not even allow us to do this, then I propose that every Sunday before those several thousand people come to our church service we will ask them to first drop off their children with you here at the police station."

The police chief did not like the idea of several thousand children being dropped off by their parents on the way to the local church, so he reluctantly agreed that the church could have a program for the children.

As of 2012, almost 250,000 Sunday school teacher-trainers had been trained in China using the Dove program. It was the first curriculum ever developed by and for the underground House Church in China.

As the Sunday school trainer program began to reach astronomical numbers, Sister Huang decided that this was her last big project in China and it was time for her to return home and retire. She walked into the boardroom during a Back to Jerusalem meeting in Austria and softly announced her plans. "It has been a great time in China and now this project is coming to a close for me," she said softly with a smile on her face that signified that she was a bit nervous. "I think that it is time for me to retire now."

The board was quiet for a moment as they pondered her announcement. The chairman of the board broke the silence by simply saying, "No."

Everyone stopped for a moment and looked up at the chairman. "No, we don't accept your retirement. The Lord is not done with you yet and neither are we. The Lord still has plans for your life and we are excited to see what is next. What God has done through you has been utterly and truly amazing, but even greater things than this are yet to come."

Dove has left the hands of the church in Wenzhou and has begun to bless other churches around the world. There are multitudes of different types of Sunday school training programs out there, so perhaps readers are wondering what makes Dove so special or different from any other programs on the market. Is it just because it is Chinese?

Listening to Sister Huang introduce it for only a few minutes will quickly make the difference apparent. The Dove training series does not merely teach children little Bible stories with cute coloring books. It is not another Sunday school program that teaches the best way to entertain children in a manner that will keep them occupied until they are back in the custody of their parents. The Dove program emphasizes the responsibility of children to become evangelists and preachers. It is structured in a way that puts the burden of missions and the Back to Jerusalem vision on the hearts of children. It is designed to teach the children how to have a direct relationship with Jesus Christ and learn to trust in Him.

In the video clip that Sister Huang often shows to introduce the Dove program, you can see children weeping before the Lord and having a genuine burden to be forgiven for their sins and be used by God. Many countries around the world have seen how this training has had such an impact on children in China and have pleaded to get it in their own languages.

As of 2012, the Dove training program has been translated into several different languages and a team from China has been sent to train Sunday school teachers in Hong Kong, Macao, Philippines, Vietnam, Ethiopia, and Egypt. The Dove training program has even been used to wake up the churches in Scandinavia and churches in Finland, Norway, and Sweden have adopted the methods used by the Chinese. The impact of Wenzhou Church on churches throughout China and around the world cannot be better seen than through the Dove training series.

19

BACK TO JERUSALEM &
THE FUTURE OF THE CHINESE HOUSE CHURCH

This chapter explores the future of the underground house churches in China and reveals more about the current status of the Back to Jerusalem vision than ever before. Since sharing about the current situation and future plans of the House Church could put others in danger, much restraint and caution has been used so the information given here is as much as can possibly be shared with the public. This information is given because those supporting the Chinese efforts from abroad need to know how better to pray for them and could even learn from their endeavors.

The origin of the underground House Church movement is rural in nature, but their future is bound to change due to the rapid urbanization of China. This phenomenon is so huge that even Wikipedia has a page devoted to it. The site claims that by the end of 2010, 49.68 percent of China's total population was living in urban areas and is expected to climb as high as seventy percent by 2035.[28]

Currently, according to our own estimates, China is nearly ten percent Christian. This number can be deceptive, because it would be obvious to anyone in China that one out of every ten people on the street there is not Christian, unless it is a place like Shandong, Anhui, or Henan. However, the estimate becomes tenable when Henan—formerly the most populated province in the nation with a high percentage of local Christians—is factored into the mix. In addition, there is a growing number of Christians in the minority areas around Guangxi, Yunnan, and Sichuan where entire people groups consider themselves to be Christian which also ups the national percentile. Since the Sichuan earthquake in 2008, the number of Christians in that area has been quickly increasing as well.

Places like Sichuan and Henan have been the most populated provinces in China for years but this has been altered in recent years. Urbanization has led to the separation of Chongqing from Sichuan Province and today Guangdong has passed up Henan as the most populated province in China. People from rural areas throughout China are racing to production powerhouse provinces like Guangdong. Large amounts of rural Christians have also started moving to the urban areas and are filling up factories, roadside shops, and office buildings throughout the cities, taking the Gospel with them.

During the twentieth century, Christianity took hold in the rural areas and spread like wildfire. The rapid rate of growth has been hard to calculate and continues in those areas even while it jumps to the urban areas. The Lord is definitely using the mass migration to the cities for His purposes. It is almost as if the Chinese evangelists were not moving fast enough to get the Gospel out of their provinces so the Lord sped up the process by sent the missionaries to a single location (the cities) and began to bring the rest of the country to them.

Until now, the general control and leadership of the House Church has been largely centralized. Urbanization is leading the churches toward more decentralized leadership. At the moment, most of the traditional networks have been focusing on aggressively evangelizing the urban areas and this has led to many groups that seem to be independent, but are not in practice.

The Five Brothers, Fangcheng, Tanghe, Blessing, Truth, and Little Joe's Network are all working in the urban areas and have planted several churches in homes, factories, and universities. Even the pastors over some of these urban groups are not always aware that their fellowship was actually a strategic plant from a major network.

As an example, suppose The Five Brothers sees a need for evangelistic outreach in Chengdu, a major city in Sichuan Province. They send a team of four evangelists and fund their efforts, who then split their efforts and focus on migrant workers and minority groups. In the migrant worker community a few older workers get saved and join a Bible study with one of the evangelists, remaining totally unaware of the fact that the evangelists are part of a much larger network. After a year, the migrant worker fellowship consists of more than fifty believers and the original migrant workers are the elders of the church actively sharing with others. After eighteen months, the Five Brothers Network re-evaluates the situation in China and decides that there is training in Thailand that they would like to send those four evangelists to participate in. Once the four evangelists graduate they will be sent to Kunming, leaving behind the churches that were set up in Chengdu to stand on their own. However, the evangelists that now live in Kunming travel regularly to the ongoing ministries in Chengdu, preach at the churches, and still guide the vision of the fledgling network, all the while taking orders from their leaders in Henan Province.

With this example, which is a common scenario in China, it is possible that the pastor of the church in Chengdu would not even know that he is part of a network in Henan Province.

As the underground House Church grows in number, it also grows in age, leaving some things open for speculation. The current leadership in most of the groups will most likely never agree to registration. There are some leaders that may be more open to it today than they were yesterday, but the majority of them refuse to register because of the obvious restrictions that registration brings.

The reasons for the refusal to register were covered earlier; however many of those reasons are linked to personal experiences. Within the underground House Church the leaders are extremely reluctant to share their personal stories. It is a strange phenomenon, that those who have been through so much and seen so many things share so little about themselves.

Joshua is one of the leaders that Back to Jerusalem International has been working with closely for several years. He has traveled to several different countries with our members and we've even shared hotel rooms together, giving us many hours to discuss all aspects of life.

However, Joshua never once mentioned some of the miracles that happened to him when he was in prison. He never speaks of how he was detained, beaten, and had his limp and broken body thrown on the floor in the prison cell, only to wake up on a bed miraculously healed with a beam of light shining down on his body from an unknown source. This miraculous light and healing led everyone in Joshua's prison cell to repent and believe in Christ. Joshua never preaches or shares openly about this testimony. Whenever we've asked him to write about it he gently says, "Maybe one day."

This is common throughout the Chinese leadership. Not many Chinese House Church pastors talk much about their past experiences. Consequently, many of the younger leaders aren't familiar with what their leaders have gone through, nor have they had to endure the same experiences. Though there is still persecution in China, it is not the same as it was twenty years ago.

The same is true of the younger leaders in government. They were not part of the generation that severely persecuted Christians. In fact, many of them have traveled to western countries and attended western universities where they were exposed to Christianity. They are not familiar with the Communism that actively and aggressively persecuted the church. In recent years government persecution of the church has been largely covered up, rather than publicized as triumphs against class enemies like in the past. Even the recent mass arrest of Shouwang Church members in Beijing for singing Christmas carols in public received more publicity outside China than within. Their society remains largely unaware of such issues because the news is not allowed to report on them.

As time goes on and members of the current generation move into primary leadership roles in the church and society, there is bound to be a policy shift in both the church and the government when it comes to ideas of registering and conducting more open activities.

Another factor that will have an increasing impact on the Chinese House Church is that Chinese are traveling more today than ever before. This exposure is giving them a different perspective about the meaning of individual freedom. If this trend continues, and there is every indicator that it will, the Chinese will continue to learn from the freedoms that they enjoy abroad and will start bringing those ideas back home.

Even when Chinese are not in a free country, they are afforded freedoms that others are not simply because they are foreigners. When Chinese travel to Egypt for example, they are free to attend a church or home prayer group without fear of harassment, things totally prohibited among the local Muslim population. The same is also true when they travel to Malaysia during Ramadan.

Even exposure to nearby places like Hong Kong, Macau, and Taiwan has had a lasting impact on Chinese who return to the mainland. These three areas have many freedoms that the Chinese do not experience in China. At first glance Hong Kong, Macau, and Taiwan seem to be exactly just a more expensive version of mainland China, but after some time it becomes more evident that these areas are very different from the mainland. They have access to foreign news, books, newspapers, and magazines that cannot be purchased in China. They are also immune to the "Great Firewall of China" and have access to all the sites blocked on the mainland, giving Chinese visitors exposure to an endless world of blogs, opinions, and social networks where people freely express themselves. Anyone familiar with the Great Firewall knows from a quick browsing session that several websites popular everywhere else in the world cannot be accessed in China. This kind of exposure is helping the younger generation shape their ideas of freedom and individuality and is changing the church as well.

The zeal of the younger generation in the underground House Church is just as strong and tenacious as that of their predecessors. This gives us reason to believe that the dedication of the church in China to carry out the Great Commission will continue for many years to come. The primary way they are doing this is through the Back to Jerusalem movement.

The unifying vision of Back to Jerusalem is showing signs of increasing in size and scope. Back to Jerusalem is most simply defined as the vision of the Chinese House Church to preach the gospel in all of the countries between the border of China and the city of Jerusalem. It is a rallying call to wake up China to become a mission-focused country.

There is excitement in the air when young people in China share about the Back to Jerusalem vision. Many Chinese see this time in history as their turn to be responsible for carrying out the Great Commission as so many others have in the past.

Many books and reports on happenings in China are about the revivals that took place in the 80s and 90s, which have led some China experts to conclude that the revivals in China are dying down and coming to a close. However, these reports usually fail to take notice of a new wind sweeping throughout China. How is most of the world missing it? Foreign Christian delegations and potential missionaries are seeing the bright lights of Shanghai, the tourist attractions in Beijing, and exploring the huge shopping areas in Shenzhen without getting a true picture of what God is going in China. Though the churches are growing at amazing rates in these cities, there are new revivals taking place in less-frequented parts of China. Places like the northeast are experiencing an awakening that has not been seen since the days of Jonathan Goforth. Young underground House Church leaders are one of the main factors contributing to those new revivals.

In August, 2010, floods struck Jilin Province. The Chinese in Jilin asked for help from foreign aid organizations, but many of them were not able to help. Many foreign Christian organizations were fatigued from other emergency aid efforts, so the Chinese church began to pool together their resources and provide aid to Jilin Province. The results have been amazing. Aid was handed out by the church while they were preaching the gospel on street corners. Believers in Jilin began to attract people from all over the province to hear the gospel, rumors of miracles began to spread, and people reported having visions like the "Macedonian call" in which they instantaneously started speaking the language of the nation calling them.

"In the city of Jilin alone we have been seeing areas with an average of fifty people per day coming to the Lord," reported one pastor involved in the relief effort.

The revivals springing up in Jilin Province are not isolated events. In December of the same year Teacher Zhao, one of Back to Jerusalem International's top teachers and administrators who has been serving in China for decades, came to Hong Kong for meetings. He had just spoken at several different churches inside China and came to give us a report on those meetings.

Teacher Zhao is from a Pentecostal background, but is rather conservative in his views and observations and is not one with a tendency to dramatize or exaggerate. If anything, the opposite could be said of him. Groups like Key Media in Finland, IBRA Radio in Sweden, AVC in Switzerland, and other large organizations around the world have relied on him for the most accurate reporting about the House Church in China.

At this particular meeting he was bubbling over with excitement as he began to describe the nature of what he had just witnessed in China. "These young people are so on fire. I haven't seen anything like it. I mean, they were crying and repenting and you could just feel the power of God. It was unlike anything I have seen before."

Less than a month later, in January of 2011, we met with

218

three leaders from the Five Brothers Network and with Little Joe. We were there to arrange for missionaries to be sent to Kazakhstan and had representatives from the local church meeting with us as well. One of the leaders, Ezekiel began to tell of what he had just experienced prior to arriving at our meeting.

In 2010 we have seen a huge revival take hold in all of China! I was there in the 1980s when China began its famous days of massive revivals, but I tell you that this revival is even stronger. This spiritual revival is happening everywhere and we have received a clear vision from God.

Before, it was our goal to train missionaries in languages and cross-cultural skills, but many of the missionaries who had been trained couldn't go because they felt too weak and incapable. Missionaries have been training all over China for years, but most of them have never had a clear vision of where to go in the Muslim, Buddhist and Communist world.

Now we are having prayer meetings where God is talking to us clearly and telling us where to go. God is specifically calling people to the western borders and to the minority groups. In the past, Chinese Back to Jerusalem missionaries would go to other countries and cultures to preach the gospel, but the vision and the calling was never really clear. The leaders often appointed people to go to different areas because of availability, not based on the calling of the Lord.

Now, believers all over China are seeing visions like the ones that the Apostle Paul had. These visions are of specific people in specific countries speaking specific languages. Some of the believers who are having these visions are even being specifically told that they will be martyred.

One night I was in western China and the Spirit of the Lord filled the room. Everyone fell to their faces and started crying and calling out to the Lord. During these meetings I couldn't sleep for two days and two nights. I couldn't stop praying. The Holy Spirit was so strong. Young people began to call out, "Yes, Lord, I am willing to die in that country for you. Yes, Lord, I am ready to have my name put into the Lamb's Book of Life."

One night, during one of these meetings a young man came to me and asked me to pray with him. I told him, "Everyone is praying. Why do you want special prayer? Just join everyone else." The young man was persistent. He told me that God told him to go to Palestine and preach the gospel, but he was afraid. He said that God was telling him clearly that Palestine will be the mission field that he will be sent to, but he was afraid of the violence towards Christians there. I told him not to fear because if God had called him, God would be with him and would strengthen him. I placed my hands on him and began to pray. After praying he replied, "God has told me clearly that I am to go to Palestine. It is there that I will be martyred, but I will not fear. I will preach the gospel of Jesus Christ because it is the Truth for all mankind. It the power that saves!"

As this young man stood there, his young wife came and stood beside him. She quoted from Ruth and said, "Where you go I will go, and where you stay I will stay. Your people will be my people and your God my God. Where you die I will die, and there I will be buried. May the Lord deal with me, be it ever so severely, if even death separates you and me." That night forty-four young people came forward and said that they too were willing to sacrifice their lives, if need be, in Muslim countries.

Revival has also been taking place in the hard to reach areas like Xinjiang. Since 2008, not many foreigners have been living in Xinjiang. Many of those who were living there prior to the Beijing Olympics were forced to leave. At that time many of them were given only forty-eight hours to sell their car and apartment, find places for their clothes and furniture, and arrange everything to get to their next destination.

Back to Jerusalem partnered with the underground House Church to help start a hotel among the Muslims in Xinjiang Province. It is one of the most difficult places to share the gospel in because there is not only aggression against Christians, but an overall hatred for Han Chinese as well.

When many of the foreigners were forced to leave in 2008, there were very few local Christians. It was not easy to find more than one or two. Today, in the small city of Kashgar and the surrounding area there is an estimated four to five hundred believers. This may not sound like a lot, but to have this many Muslims come to Christ in such a short time is evidence of an amazing revival among the Muslims in western China.

These revivals are getting Christians excited about the new role of China and the Back to Jerusalem vision. The vision has a flavor that is unique to the Chinese. The impact that God is having on China and the spiritual fruit of Chinese serving around the world is already very visible.

The future and longevity of the Chinese House Church can better be understood by looking at firsthand information from Back to Jerusalem missionaries working in other countries. Here is rare information on just a few countries that they are working in now.

Bhutan

Many people have never heard about the country of Bhutan, hidden in the Himalayas. It is sandwiched between the two giants of China and India. For generations this country actually lied about their population, keeping it artificially inflated to discourage being invaded by their neighbors. Back to Jerusalem has been working closely with the underground church in Bhutan. Representatives from Back to Jerusalem were present at the meeting between Paro and Thimpu that took place in 2006 to establish the Christian Alliance of Bhutan.

The nature of the project together with the Chinese underground missionaries cannot be given in detail here, but the Chinese are using their experiences in Tibet to relate, connect, and serve the church of Bhutan.

North Korea

Back to Jerusalem missionaries have been working inside North Korea since 2007. Not many countries have as close a relationship with North Korea as China maintains. Today several Back to Jerusalem missionaries are living and working in North Korea, preaching the gospel and using small electronic Bibles to help spread the Word.

In April of 2011 alone, Back to Jerusalem missionaries were

able to produce and deliver one thousand handheld video players that were preloaded with several hours of Christian movies, gospel teaching, and an entire audio Bible in their native dialect. At the end of that October, another thousand were sent in.

During that year, Back to Jerusalem missionaries were also able to deliver food to starving families located throughout North Korea. Food distribution is not an easy task and large donations are often redirected to the military or government officials, but it is something that the Chinese are better able to monitor and they are dedicated to doing so to help share the love of Christ.

Sudan

In September of 2011, the first Chinese Back to Jerusalem missionary traveled to the world's newest country: South Sudan. South Sudan was officially recognized as a free independent nation on July 9, 2011. The road to independence has been a long and hard one. Christians have a history of being severely persecuted by the Muslims in Sudan. According to Wikipedia, more than 1.5 million Christians have been killed in Sudan since 1984 and other sources would actually put the number at more than two million.[29]

Sudan was one of the first countries in the world to provide slaves to other nations. Today Africans from Sudan are still being sold as slaves and the news media outlets around the world continue to refuse to report on it. While Chinese Back to Jerusalem missionaries were visiting South Sudan, they were able to spend much of their time with the Dinka tribe. The enslavement of the Dinkas in Southern Sudan may be one of the most horrific well-known examples of contemporary slavery in the world. Joshua, the Chinese House Church pastor mentioned several times before in this book, was greatly moved by the church in this area. According to official reports, there may be as many as ninety-thousand Africans from Sudan who are owned by Arab Muslims. They have been sold as property for as little as US $15 per person.[30]

After spending some time in Sudan, the Chinese evangelists said, "We believe that God is moving mightily in this country. Sudan played an important role in the beginning times and they will play an important role in the end times. We must return the hate of the Muslims with the love of Christ. We must stand with our persecuted brothers and sisters in Sudan and let them know that they are not defeated and they are not alone. The church in China stands together with them and we will not only say it with our words, we are willing to display it with our actions."

At the time of writing, six Back to Jerusalem missionaries are in training with the goal of moving to Sudan permanently in 2012.

Nepal

Today there are a couple of teams made up of more than twenty missionaries who are living and working in Nepal. A few of them were trained at our base in the Philippines. The team serving there now has also passed through one of the main vocational training programs in Tibet that is run by Back to Jerusalem.

Prior to their departure for Nepal, we met with them and listened to their challenges and concerns. It was important that they knew what to expect because other Back to Jerusalem missionaries had encountered difficulties in that country that discouraged and shocked them. The previous missionary couple, who moved to Nepal in 2007, did well for the first part of the year but after a while the living conditions there became very challenging for them. When the wife became pregnant, they left Nepal and returned to China. They have not been back since.

The team that is there now is actively studying the language and working in the open market to share the gospel.

India

India is the top destination for most Back to Jerusalem missionaries in China—at least in theory. At any given Bible school, one can ask the students what country they feel called to and most of the time India will be the response of the majority of the class.

The main reason for this is that most Back to Jerusalem missionaries have not been formally educated and have never been to secondary school. India is really the only other country that many of them know or have heard anything about.

We have traveled with Chinese missionaries and leaders to India, but have yet to see a team settle there for the long term. In 2012, a team of four missionaries will travel there to work with an agricultural business and will use that business as an avenue for preaching the gospel.

Tanzania

Back to Jerusalem missionaries were sent from China to Tanzania and have successfully helped serve the local church there for more than four years. These Chinese missionaries started off as assistants in an orphanage and then began serving the international church.

Pakistan

Pakistan shares a border with China and is actively engaging China for a broader partnership. Pakistan sees China as key in their rivalry with India and likes to court the Chinese whenever possible.

Ten Back to Jerusalem missionaries have been working and serving in Pakistan for two years in three different locations. They have just finished their language training and are actively serving the church. Back to Jerusalem missionaries have also sent in hundreds of audio Bibles in Urdu, the local language, that are being used to teach the Bible to illiterate Christians and for Muslim evangelism.

Egypt

Back to Jerusalem missionaries have set up businesses in Egypt and are serving there today even amongst the political turmoil. These missionaries have utilized a wonderful idea for business that allows them to have daily interaction with Muslim women who are not permitted to leave their homes without a male escort.

The Chinese missionaries have engaged them and are able to minister to them in a unique way. During a trip to Egypt, our representatives were able to enjoy a meal on the Nile River with a team of Back to Jerusalem missionaries. We also spent time with a local Muslim whom the Chinese missionaries had befriended. This local resident was more of a cultural Muslim than a practicing one and was very open to the gospel, even joining us in prayer before our meal.

The Chinese have seen a few people in Egypt come to the

Lord. Today there are about twenty Back to Jerusalem missionaries from China living and working in Egypt.

Syria

Since terrible domestic turmoil began in Syria, there have been fewer and fewer missionaries left there to share the gospel. However, Chinese Back to Jerusalem workers are still ministering in this country. They were able to set up a small business from the training provided at one of the Back to Jerusalem training centers. Today there are five Back to Jerusalem missionaries still living and serving in Syria.

Iran

Back to Jerusalem missionaries are currently highly motivated and focused on the country of Iran. In 2011, Back to Jerusalem partners were successful in printing and delivery of thirty thousand Bibles to this nation. China's House Church networks are concentrating their efforts on moving into Iran and its neighboring countries in order to bring the gospel to the people of ancient Persia. The goal for 2012 is to send fifteen missionaries to Iran and its bordering countries.

Cambodia

Today there are ten Back to Jerusalem missionaries ministering in Cambodia. Half of them are working for an American clothing brand. The boss of the company in Cambodia is a believer and uses this platform to provide visas for the Chinese. The American side of the company has no clue that their factory is being used for this purpose.

Half of the missionaries there are from one House Church network in Henan and the other half is from a network in Anhui. These two groups are working completely independent from one another.

The group from Anhui spent the first year learning the language and the second year living in small villages to learn more about the language and culture. The third year they were commissioned by their home church to start a church. They ended up starting three churches in the first six months.

Laos

There are currently five Back to Jerusalem missionaries living and working in Laos. They have opened a service business to serve the local community and are using that business as their platform.

Places like Laos are easier for the Chinese to transition to because there are buses from China to Laos and many of the imported products are directly from the mainland. Most of the locals have been working with Chinese businessmen for generations so there is already a natural connection.

This is not an exhaustive list of Back to Jerusalem projects. There are more missionaries living, working, training, and preaching abroad than we are aware of. It is impossible to know exactly what every network is doing in every country. Back to Jerusalem missionaries are also in countries like Yemen, Vietnam, and Ethiopia. There are actually more Chinese missionaries living in Myanmar than in any other country.

This list also doesn't take into account the large number of Chinese Christians living abroad that aren't officially missionaries. Thousands of Chinese who had never been exposed to Christianity in China are getting saved in 10/40 Window nations on a regular basis. A sister in Guangdong Province who now oversees the production of many of the Back to Jerusalem electronics became a Christian while working for a company in Saudi Arabia.

At a Christian home group in Egypt, we met a group of Chinese who were all working for foreign companies there. The group of about fifteen people had all come to Christ while living in Cairo.

By looking at the past and present situation of the underground House Church and identifying obvious patterns and trends, it is possible to make some projections regarding its future. Considering the urbanization, transformation, and globalization of China and the House Church movement, it is clear that the movement will continue to expand and to bring the message of Christ to every tribe, tongue, and nation between China and Jerusalem.

20

CONCLUSION

As was discussed in previous chapters of this book, the last few decades of Chinese church history were largely directed by the great work of God flowing out of Nanyang. A foreign visitor to that area would most likely look around and immediately wonder why God would choose such a place to pour out His grace. Nanyang is about ten years behind the rest of China in many ways. It does not contain any notable foreign communities and any foreigner visiting there is stared at and sometimes pointed out by local children shouting, "*Laowai!*" ("old foreigner" in Chinese).

One House Church worker from the Five Brothers Network described Nanyang this way, "There are four areas of unrest for the Chinese government: Taiwan, Xinjiang, Tibet, and Nanyang." It is hard to imagine that this county has had such an impact on the entire world.

Uncovering the Chinese House Church's mysteries can help Christians in other countries and cultures reflect on their own relationships with Jesus Christ. The history and testimonies of the underground Chinese believers are encouraging because they show us what God can do in a country that declares war on His people like the Chinese government did. China declared war on the Christians, but Jesus never left them. He never abandoned the Chinese people and is actually using them today in amazing ways to fulfill the Great Commission.

Looking into the secrets of the Chinese House Church can also shock us into seeing the Bible without using the cultural spectacles that sometimes dilute and pervert the Word of God. At first glance, several elements of the Chinese House Church might look like the result of bad judgment, but upon closer evaluation many of these elements are actually closer to the Jewish culture Jesus grew up in than the western culture that dominates most foreign churches.

In this book we have explored the history of the underground House Church, identified the main networks within the movement, and explained the different elements that have helped propel the growth of the underground House Church. Examples and personal testimonies play important roles in bringing history alive and have thus been included sporadically. It is in these personal trials and memories that we can better understand concepts and situations that are completely foreign to outsiders.

After evaluating the hidden treasures of the underground House Church and looking at some of the secrets that are mostly unknown to the rest of the world, we stumble across at least nine characteristics that are unique to the Chinese House Church and have contributed to its growth in one way or another.

1. Persecution

Persecution is not unique to the Chinese underground House Church. If persecution was indeed the only requirement for a revival then China would not be alone in seeing massive numbers of people come to the Lord. However, the Chinese persecutions have been unique in that the government actually implemented a plan for the systematic destruction of the church in China.

Chinese persecution was a direct assault on the Christian leadership in China and aimed to erase the name of Jesus from Chinese soil forever. Christians were not merely a by-product of massive widespread effort to stamp out all political opponents of Communism, but were specifically singled out for destruction.

In fact, many Christians and church leaders in China initially agreed with and supported the tenets of Communism. The Communist Party of China had the support of many Christians who were happy to see the tyrannical Nationalists replaced by those who claimed to support equal distribution of wealth and resources. In theory, equal distribution was already being practiced by indigenous Christian groups like the Jesus Family and the Back to Jerusalem Evangelistic Band in the 1940s. The Communist Party of China had an early ally in this regard.

It was the Party that first viewed the church as a natural enemy. The persecution in China did not only inflict pain on Christians, but was an attempt to pollute, dilute, pervert, and completely destroy the church. The government persecuted the church with a rarely observed vile hatred that can only be explained as demonic in nature.

The enemy saw the future and potential of the Chinese church. The history of Sino-Christianity was determined by the Lord's changeless will and the enemy moved to prevent it. Could the enemy have predicted that the very acts used to eradicate Christianity would be instrumental in bringing about church growth that would not have been possible otherwise?

2. Mao Zedong

Mao Zedong was unique to China and despite all of his anti-Christian propaganda, hideous orders of destruction upon the church, and systematic attacks on Christian beliefs, he undeniably put into place the very factors needed to assist, nurture, and facilitate the growth of the world's largest revival.

He insisted that everyone in the country become responsible for the sins of their neighbors. Confession sessions were arranged for the Chinese to come forward with valuable, self-incriminating information about themselves or their neighbors. It was everyone's responsibility to know if their neighbors were involved in foul play, creating a very open society.

According to Mao Zedong, you are your brother's keeper. The confession sessions were implemented to create an atmosphere of fear where no one would ever attempt to go against the Communist Party for fear of being caught by family, friends, or neighbors who in turn were afraid not to report an illegal activity for fear that they too would get in trouble. This created the perfect environment for healings and other miracles of God to be witnessed and shared. In such a confessional society news spread very quickly, even the Good News.

Chairman Mao also standardized the Mandarin language for everyone in China, making it possible to get the gospel out to many people without having to learn other languages. This removed a huge barrier that hadn't been possible to overcome before.

Mao also connected the country with a road and railway system that made it possible for missionaries and evangelists to quickly travel around preaching the Word of God to everyone that would listen. Developing the transportation system allowed the gospel to spread through and between provinces faster than ever before.

3. Miracles

When exploring the roots of the House Church revivals, we find a serious lack of Bibles, teachers, Christian materials, and other resources traditionally utilized to share the Word. One thing that was not lacking, however, was God's presence. His fingerprints can be found all over the churches in Henan and Anhui where many people were healed and witnessed miracles.

It is easy to deny rational teachings and moving speeches, or to respond cynically to a religious book, but it is much more difficult to deny the power of God in action. It is also much harder to deny a God who answers desperate prayers when every other option had been exhausted and there is no other hope.

Those dying from disease and starvation had no one to turn to for help. The sick had no places to go for treatment. Many of them turned to Jesus as a last resort and found mercy, rest, and supernatural healing through God's power.

Rumors of healing and other miracles spread like wildfire throughout the Chinese countryside. When people were healed, they couldn't help but tell everyone what had happened to them. When others were sick and had no hope they turned to the same Jesus who so many others had turned to and found hope and relief.

When believers prayed for simple things like Bibles, God would miraculously answer their prayers. When they prayed for safety, God protected them. When they asked for freedom from prison, God sometimes opened the iron gates of the correctional fortresses and let His servants walk out free. The early revivals in Henan and Anhui were fueled by the testimonies of many miracles.

4. Charismatic Faith

The early movements of the underground House Church were not propelled or supported by academia. Even today, the rough and crude farmers in China who are part of the underground House Church movement are not accepted by theological academics.

The prayers lifted up at an average House Church meeting are not read from a piece of paper prepared in advance like in some formal western denominations, but are marked with passionate, impromptu cries and bold proclamations.

The gifts of the Holy Spirit are widely accepted and practiced, but certain activities like speaking in tongues and prophesying are not emphasized. Impromptu dancing and singing during prayer and worship times are encouraged and done with great joy, but are quite natural to the culture and not at all distracting like they would be in most western church settings. There is nothing really formal or stuffy about worship in the underground House Church.

What makes the charismatic element unique in China is that it is not disorderly. One of the biggest accusations made by those opposed to charismatic worship is the disorder and chaos it can create, but that is not the case in China. Even though it is done without planning or strategic leading, it is nonetheless done together. If one person is singing and dancing in a room full of people praying at an underground meeting, everyone is singing and dancing along with them. If one person is on their knees, crying and shouting out prayers, the entire room will begin to do the same. The charismatic activities are individual and unique to every person within the church, but yet somehow orderly and in unison as one body.

5. Female Leadership

One of the obvious characteristics of the Chinese House Church is the overwhelming percentage of women in the movement. The vast majority of evangelists and missionaries who are trained and sent to the field are young women. To ignore the dominant role that women have played and how much they have contributed to church growth would be deliberate ignorance.

Although none of the top leaders of the traditional networks are female, many of the movers and shakers in individual churches are. These women have made their mark on the largest revival in history as well as the largest ever missionary movement.

The women serve in the background and do so swiftly and effectively, doing more in a short period of time than men who might expect to be rewarded for their efforts. They don't ask for recognition, in fact they shun it, but they work as if they are working for the Father.

The women in the underground House Church movement

will often set up for a meeting, preach the sermon, feed the attendees, and clean up after everyone has departed. They are self-sacrificing warriors and heroes and collectively are one of the main reasons for the rapid growth of Christianity in China.

6. Absence of Foreign Denominations

Foreign missions need to be credited with planting the seeds of the gospel in China. Fruit is still being produced thanks to the past efforts of foreign missionaries who toiled to till the soil of Chinese hearts. However, their presence, followed by their absence had more of an impact than could have been imagined. Their continued presence, coupled with stifling control measures would have undoubtedly had a negative impact on church growth.

Parents are needed while a child is growing up. Love, attention, devotion, and sacrifice are all a part of bringing up a small child. However, when those parents become overbearing and don't allow a child to make his or her own decisions, the consequences can be disastrous for the maturation process of the child.

Missionaries and mission organizations often have a hard time with the final phase of mission work. Recognizing the child as an equal when they are fully grown is often delayed. China was able to sever the umbilical cord of foreign funding the hard way. The separation process was difficult for the Chinese and it was equally challenging for the missionaries. No one would have willingly chosen the road that the underground House Church has had to travel on, nor would anyone have willingly accepted the fire that the underground House Church has had to go through. However, out of that forced separation came a church that is now independent, self-sustaining, and thriving in an environment that makes it possible for the Chinese and foreign churches to maintain a healthy relationship of mutual respect and support.

7. Paternal Leadership

Leaders in China are regarded as parental figures. Their opinions are revered and their commands are obeyed. This leadership style may not work well in western culture, but the current church growth would have never happened without it.

Being able to give orders and know that they will be

followed without question has allowed the leaders to manage an army of believers in China that are ready to march on the gates of hell. This army strongly believes in its cause and completely trusts its leaders. Naturally there are flaws with this kind of leadership model, as with any, but it has been very advantageous for the Chinese. Whether we agree with it or not, this is the model that the Chinese use and the one that God has chosen to work mightily through.

8. Back to Jerusalem

The Great Commission compelled the early church to go into unknown lands to share the Good News. From the first missionary expeditions of Paul and Barnabas to today's thriving missionary organizations, the Great Commission has sent missionaries into far-flung lands under less than desirable conditions to bring people out of darkness and despair.

The Back to Jerusalem vision of the underground church in China is to take the gospel into the countries between the borders of China and Jerusalem. That swath of land contains the highest level of poverty and the largest number of unreached people groups on earth today. Despite the desperate need there, only a small percentage of mission funds from the western world are used to evangelize this area.

This situation is changing with the Chinese. As the Chinese House Church increases its numbers, so also do its missionaries. Unlike most of the western church, their focus is on the hardest to reach areas. Their missionaries are being sent to the most difficult countries and the majority of their resources are being used for this effort.

Back to Jerusalem has been the heart cry of the Chinese church for several generations, but only a handful of believers carried it through the darkest hours of persecution. Today the younger generation has caught the vision and is determined to carry out the mission. With a strong unifying vision, the younger generation has a direct passion to funnel their energy and efforts into this task. In many Christian circles around the world today, the passion for the Great Commission has been lost and as a result we see that western society in general is becoming more secular.

The question can be asked, "Is the mission focus not as

strong because society has become more secular or is society more secular because the vision for mission has been lost by the church?" It seems to be the latter. A church without vision lacks the inspiration and direction to make any real impact on society. A new day has dawned in China and a fresh vision has come to life. The vision lay dormant for decades but has awakened and is now being passed from person to person with excitement and zeal.

Even for outsiders, the Back to Jerusalem vision of the Chinese House Church is exciting because of what it represents: the rise and global impact of a church thought to have been wiped out by the Chinese Communist regime. It also represents the power of God to reach down and breathe life into absolute darkness in open defiance of what everyone thought to be true. It represents a new wave that has been ordained to defy racist statements made by missiologists of past generations who thought the world could only be reached by western missionaries. The Back to Jerusalem vision is the unique Chinese version of the Great Commission that God is using to usher in the imminent return of Jesus Christ.

9. The Holy Spirit

In many ways, the Holy Spirit trumps all the other elements previously mentioned. If a sterile environment were to be created in which all the elements and unique characteristics listed above were added, revival still could not be recreated by man. Only the timing and movement of the Holy Spirit could have transformed the church in China in the ways we have seen. The Holy Spirit, for whatever reason, has chosen China to be used during this age. This special act of God's sovereign will makes the underground House Church in China unique.

These nine characteristics are by no means exhaustive, but just a few elements that have made the underground House Church unique and can help us understand why they are experiencing the world's largest revival and focusing on the world's largest missionary movement.

This revival will be hard to stop. Attacks cannot be merely targeted at the leadership. The leaders have already designated replacements throughout China who are completely capable of maintaining the current levels of activity.

These replacements are currently involved in training, administration, security, personnel logistics, fundraising, and material distribution. They mostly operate with a great deal of autonomy in executing projects because security issues prevent them from directly communicating with their leadership on a regular basis. They have very little autonomy when choosing direction and vision, but a lot of freedom to carry out orders once they have been given.

The underground House Church is mobile and hard for the authorities to follow and observe on a regular basis. This is largely because they don't have a headquarters. There is no large facility that can be attacked, raided, monitored, or razed to the ground. Any facility used for logistical missions like Bible deliveries is rented on a month-to-month basis utilizing fake identification cards and disposable phone numbers that can quickly be discarded.

After examining the underground House Church, one cannot help but be amazed at what God is doing in the world today. It is amazing that there are no dominant personalities in the movement who lead the charge for their own personal gain. Each leader within this movement in China is mostly guaranteed a life of persecution, hardship, imprisonment, and sometimes even martyrdom.

When we uncover the mysteries of the House Church networks we soon discover that most of the time they were built on the backs of people seeking relief from poverty, sickness, and death. The people who make up these mysterious underground churches had an illness or a dear family member with one and saw Christ miraculously move in a way that changed them forever.

It is quite interesting that Chinese Christians who found Jesus in most desperate circumstances became passionate about following Him even to death despite not knowing much other than His power to save and heal. In the West, where we have access to so much information and Bible knowledge, we can easily live our entire lives absolutely passionless before Christ.

The underground church in China seems to be built on a mixture of ignorance and blind faith, but that blind faith is anchored in their Savior, Jesus Christ. Western churches in general seem to be built on the confidence of their own understanding of the Word of God and rationalism, relying more on tangible and reasonably attainable goals.

At the banks of the Red Sea with a furious Egyptian army at their backs, God commanded Moses to take all the people of Israel across, "Lift up your staff, and stretch out your hand over the sea and divide it, that the people of Israel may go through the sea on dry ground" (Exodus 14:16).

If that command were given to us today what would be our reaction? Would we rely on our own abilities or would we trust in the power of God? Would we put a committee together to discuss how to go about obeying the command? Would we try to find some more "practical" way to cross the sea other than the directions already given by God?

Or would we, with total faith and complete abandonment of our own feeble wisdom, scrap the idea of a committee and the other plans and simply lift our staff and cross the sea as God commanded, trusting in Him to perform a miracle?

The Chinese House Church didn't have a choice, but had to accept the latter. May we all learn to trust more in the Lord than ever before by seeing what God has done and continues to do in China. May we all stop looking at the teachings of the Word of God through the limited scope of our own cultures. May the mysteries that have brought the underground House Church in China through the most turbulent time in China's history teach us to rely on God always for everything. If the Sovereign Creator of the universe can use the evil schemes of man to bring about the greatest spiritual harvest in history, surely He can provide for us as we walk in obedience to Him one day at a time.

NOTES

1. Davy Tong and Raymond Petzholdt, The True Spiritual Roots for All Chinese (Davy Tong and Raymond Petzholt, 2000).

2. Don Richardson, Eternity in Their Hearts, rev. ed. (Ventura, CA: Regal Books, 1984), 62-67.

3. An excellent book on this subject is Ethel R. Nelson, Richard E. Broadberry, and Ginger Tong Chock, God's Promise to the Chinese (Great Britain: Read Books Publisher, 1997).

4. Paul Hattaway, Back to Jerusalem: Three Chinese House Church Leaders Share Their Vision to Complete the Great Commission (Carlisle, UK: Piquant editions, 2003), 4-5.

5. A. J. Broomhall, The Shaping of Modern China: Hudson Taylor's Life and Legacy, Vol. 1: Early-1867, 2nd ed. (Carlisle, UK: Piquant editions, 2005), 8-11.

6. Ibid., 38-43.

7. Dr. and Mrs. Howard Taylor, Hudson Taylor's Spiritual Secret (Chicago: Moody Press, 1989), 62.

8. A. J. Broomhall, The Shaping of Modern China: Hudson Taylor's Life and Legacy, Vol. 2: 1867-1990, 2nd ed. (Carlisle, UK: Piquant editions, 2005), 754.

9. Ibid., 755.

10. China News and Church Report, September 15, 1997.

11. Eugene Back and Brother Zhu, The Heavenly People: Going underground with Brother Yun and the Chinese House Church (Blountsville, AL: The Fifth Estate, 2011).

12. David Aikman, Jesus in Beijing: How Christianity Is Transforming China and Changing the Global Balance of Power (Washington, DC: Regnery Publishing, Inc., 2006), 213.

13. Anna Louise Strong, Tibetian Inverviews (New World Press, 1959), 76-78.

14. These are excerpts from a translated testimony written by Shen Xiaoming and used with his permission.

15. Personal interview with Pastor Chen in June 2011

16. Most of the information for this chapter is from a personal interview with Sister H in February, 2012.

17. Personal interview with Joshua in Shenzhen on February 3, 2012

18. Brother Yun and Paul Hattaway, The Heavenly Man: The Remarkable True Story of Chinese Christian Brother Yun (London: Monarch Books, 2002), 233.

19. Ibid., 237.

20. "Luis Palau issues statement after China comments disputed," Baptist Press, accessed February 25, 2012, http://www.bpnews.net/bpnews.asp?id=22173.

21. "China Trip Successful," accessed on February 25, 2012, http://www.palau.org/news/story/china_trip_successful_ 344.

22. Tim Funk, "Graham Discourages 'Illegal' Evangelizing in China," CovenantNews.com, accessed February 25, 2012, http://www.covenantnews.com/newswire/archives/042879.html.

23. Wikipedia contributors, "State Religious Affairs Bureau Order No. 5," Wikipedia, The Free Encyclopedia, accessed February 25, 2012, http://en.wikipedia.org/w/index.php?title=State_Religious_Affairs_Bureau_Order_No._5&oldid=456925752.

24. Personal interview with Little Joe in shanghai in June 2011.

25. Luke Leung, "Author of 'Canaan Hymns' Xiao Min Gave Touching Testimony of Faith," The Gospel Herald, accessed February 25, 2012, http://www.gospelherald.net/article/ministries/44870/author-of-canaan-hymns-xiao-min-gave-touching-testimony-of-faith.htm.

26. Paul Hattaway, Henan: The Galilee of China (Carlisle, UK: Piquant editions, 2009), 219.

27. Nicholas D. Kristof, "Christianity Is Booming In China Despite Rifts," The New York Times online; NYTimes.com, accessed February 25, 2012, http://www.nytimes.com/1993/02/07/world/christianity-is-booming-in-china-despite-rifts.html?pagewanted=all&src=pm.

28. Wikipedia contributors, "Urbanization in the People's Republic of China," Wikipedia, The Free Encyclopedia, accessed February 20, 2012, http://en.wikipedia.org/w/index.php?title=Urbanization_in_the_People%27s_Republic_of_China&oldid=472785000.

29. Wikipedia contributors, "Persecution of Christians," Wikipedia, The Free Encyclopedia, accessed February 20, 2012, http://en.wikipedia.org/w/index.php?title=Persecution_of_Christians&oldid=477766839.

30. "Slavery in the Modern World." Infoplease. Accessed February 20, 2012, http://www.infoplease.com/spot/slavery1.html.